Laura Porter writes AboutLondonLaura.com and contributes to many other publications while maintaining an impressive afternoon tea addiction. You can find Laura on Twitter as @AboutLondon and on Facebook as @AboutLondonLaura.

There's plenty going on in the capital in 2022. Do remember, even free museums and galleries are likely to continue requiring pre-booking. And note that South Kensington tube station is closed on the Piccadilly line platform until March 2022 (but is open for the Circle and District lines). On 31 August 2022 it will be 25 years since the death of Diana, Princess of Wales so we can expect more events to commemorate that date.

STILL ON FROM 2021

Masterpieces from Buckingham Palace

The Queen's Gallery; 4 December 2020 – 13 February 2022
Nearest Station: Victoria

Admire spectacular paintings widely recognized as among the highlights of the Royal Collection including works by Titian, Rembrandt, Rubens, Vermeer, Van Dyck and Canaletto. These are 65 of the most treasured paintings that usually hang in the Picture Gallery at Buckingham Palace. The more intimate display at The Queen's Gallery gives audiences the chance to enjoy each painting up close, inviting them to consider what made these works astonishing at the time of their creation, what they can offer a modern viewer and why these paintings deserve to be described as 'masterpieces'.
www.rct.uk

Our Broken Planet: How We Got Here and Ways to Fix It

Natural History Museum; December 2020 – 18 April 2022
Nearest tube: South Kensington

Explore how humanity has affected the planet and how scientists are finding solutions from nature for nature. Opening throughout the year in three stages, the free display highlights some fantastic species and how our actions are affecting them. From a humongous 3m long black marlin skeleton to the wild and now-extinct ancestor of cows; visitors can get up close and personal to a variety of creatures from the Museum's world-leading collection.
www.nhm.ac.uk

Laughing Matters: The State of a Nation 2021

V&A; 29 March 2021 – 29 March 2022
Nearest Station: South Kensington

Through more than 30 objects, ranging from costumes to scripts, from puppets to music, this display unpicks the punchlines to discover what humour since the Victorian era – whether subversive, surreal, mocking or celebratory – can tell us about what it means to be British today.
vam.ac.uk

Our Future Planet

Science Museum; 19 May 2021 – 4 September 2022
Nearest Station: South Kensington

Alongside global efforts to urgently reduce greenhouse gas emissions, scientists are racing to develop different technologies to remove and store excess carbon dioxide—the most significant cause of climate change. This free exhibition is the first significant UK exhibition to be presented on the subject of carbon capture and storage. It showcases the cutting-edge technology and nature-based solutions being developed to trap carbon dioxide released by human activity, notably the burning of fossil fuels.
www.sciencemuseum.org.uk

LONDON IN 2022

Your Guide to the Sights, Sounds, and Events Awaiting You in London in 2022

By Laura Porter

Table of Contents

About the Magazine

The London Annual is published once a year by Anglotopia LLC, a USA registered Corporation. All contents copyrighted.

Letters to the Editors may be addressed to:

Anglotopia LLC
8 The Green
Suite 5331
Dover, DE 19901

On Point: Royal Academy of Dance at 100

V&A; June 2021 – 1 May 2022
Nearest Station: South Kensington

Explore the 100-year history of the prestigious Royal Academy of Dance. Discover a host of costume, designs, film and unique material from the last century including shoes worn by Dame Darcey Bussell DBE at her 2007 farewell performance.
vam.ac.uk

A Year in Art: Australia 1922

Tate Modern; 8 June 2021 – Spring 2022
Nearest Station: Southwark

This free exhibition brings together works that respond to debates around Aboriginal and Torres Strait Islander land rights in Australia. It takes as its starting point the landmark 1992 High Court ruling in favour of Torres Strait Islander land-rights activist Edward Koiki Mabo. The ruling overturned terra nullius (meaning 'land belonging to no-one'), the doctrine on which the British justified colonising the land now known as Australia. The exhibition explores how artists have acknowledged the continuing relationship Aboriginal and Torres Strait Islander peoples have with their lands, as well as the ongoing impact of colonisation and the complexities of representation in Australian society today.
www.tate.org.uk

Yayoi Kusama: Infinity Mirror Rooms

Tate Modern; 14 June 2021 – 12 June 2022
Nearest Station: Southwark

By one of the most celebrated artists working today, this is a rare chance to experience two of these much-loved immersive installations that transport the viewer into the artist's unique vision of endless reflections. Alongside is fascinating early documentation of Kusama's experimental performances and events, as well as a brand-new sculptural work that continues the theme of endless replication.
www.tate.org.uk

Major refresh of the V&A's Theatre and Performance Galleries

V&A; between August 2021 and April 2022
Nearest Station: South Kensington

Several significant costumes including an iconic drag costume from the musical 'Kinky Boots' (2012), Eurovision winner Sandie Shaw's mini dress and the UK's first ballet pointe shoes for a variety of skin tones by Freed / Ballet Black have gone on display as part of a major refresh in these museum galleries. With a rolling programme of new material on display each month, the refresh introduces over 120 objects from the V&A's Theatre and Performance collection into the galleries, the majority of which are on display for the first time.
vam.ac.uk

Emery Walker and the Private Press Movement

Emery Walker's House; 12 August 2021 – 30 May 2022
Nearest Station: Stamford Brook

The first exhibition ever held here displays examples of stunning private press books illustrating Walker's revolutionary book printing techniques and legacy. Entry to the exhibition is included in the guided tours of the house and riverside garden. The new exhibition space is in the small drawing room of what is claimed to be the most authentic Arts & Crafts home in Britain.
www.emerywalker.org.uk

Frans Hals: The Male Portrait

Wallace Collection; 22 September 2021 – 30 January 2022
Nearest Station: Bond Street

Frans Hals's most famous and beloved painting,

'The Laughing Cavalier', painted in 1624 has been in the Wallace Collection since 1865. This iconic image has never been seen together with other works by the artist so is the centrepiece of the exhibition that focuses solely on Hals's portraits of men posing on their own. It explores his highly innovative approach to male portraiture in particular, from the beginning of his career in the 1610s until the end of his life in 1666 with a careful selection of the artist's best male portraits from Europe and North America.
www.wallacecollection.org

Romeo & Juliet The Musical

Shaftesbury Theatre; 24 September 2021 – 12 February 2022
Nearest Station: Tottenham Court Road

Full of pop anthems, incredible sets and electrifying choreography, this West End musical retells Shakespeare's classic tale of Romeo & Juliet. Discover what life would have been like for Juliet beyond Romeo, had she been able to choose her own future. The story of Juliet's life after love is told through some of the catchiest pop songs from the last 30 years. Hits include Baby One More Time, Since U Been Gone, Roar and Everybody (Backstreet's Back) – all composed by legendary songwriter Max Martin.
www.andjulietthemusical.co.uk

Hokusai: The Great Picture Book of Everything

British Museum; 30 September 2021 – 30 January 2022
Nearest Station: Tottenham Court Road

See a collection of rare drawings by Katsushika Hokusai – one of Japan's most celebrated artists, best known for his iconic print 'Under the Wave off Kanagawa' popularly called 'The Great Wave'. In a world-first, this exhibition displays 103 recently acquired drawings produced in the 1820s–1840s for an illustrated encyclopedia called 'The Great Picture Book of Everything'. For reasons unknown the book was never published, presenting the opportunity to see these exceptional works which would otherwise have been destroyed as part of the woodblock printing process.
www.britishmuseum.org

Noguchi

Barbican Art Gallery; 30 September 2021 – 9 January 2022
Nearest Station: Barbican

Japanese American sculptor Isamu Noguchi (1904–1988) is one of the most experimental and important artists of the twentieth century. This is the first European touring retrospective of his work in 20 years. Retracing the evolution of Noguchi's kaleidoscopic career over six decades across sculpture, architecture, dance and design, the exhibition celebrates the artist's inventive and risk-taking approach to sculpture as a living environment. The exhibition brings together over 150 works, including an extraordinary range of sculptures – created in stone, bronze, ceramics, wood, aluminium and galvanised steel – as well as theatre set designs, architectural and playground models, lighting and furniture design.
www.barbican.org.uk

Beano: The Art of Breaking Rules

Somerset House; 21 October 2021 – 6 March 2022
Nearest Station: Temple

This landmark show celebrates the world's longest-running weekly comic's mix of mischief, mayhem and fun, and explores the under-acknowledged influence of comics on today's greatest creative rule-breakers, including writers, musicians, painters, sculptors and photographers.
www.somersethouse.org.uk

**Beautiful People: The Boutique in
1960s Counterculture**
Fashion & Textile Museum; 1 October 2021 –
13 March 2022
Nearest Station: London Bridge

In the mid-1960s a handful of Chelsea
boutiques sparked a fashion revolution
selling radical clothing to the counterculture
youth. Their outrageously flamboyant designs
were inspired by romantic ideas of the past,
blurred gender boundaries with increasingly
androgynous styles, while creating an explosion
of colour, pattern and decoration. The
exhibition explores fabulous and rare examples
from these era-defining stores and designers.
Designs worn by the likes of The Beatles, The
Rolling Stones and Jimi Hendrix are on display
as part of recreations of these iconic boutiques.
www.ftmlondon.org

Mamma Mia! The Party
O2 Arena; 1 October 2021 – 3 April 2022
Nearest Station: North Greenwich

Featuring Abba's catchy hits, this new story
explores the lives of residents of Skopelos,
where the first Mamma Mia! movie was shot.
The story revolves around a love affair, adapted
by British writer Sandi Toksvig.
www.theo2.co.uk

Shilpa Gupta
The Curve, Barbican Centre; 7 October 2021 –
6 February 2022
Nearest Station: Barbican

One of South Asia's most critically acclaimed
artists working today, Gupta's multidisciplinary
practice encompasses a wide range of media
and processes, from text, sculpture, video,
photography, and sound which poetically
explores physical and ideological boundaries
and how, as individuals, we come to feel a sense
of isolation or belonging.
www.barbican.org.uk

Amazônia
Science Museum; 13 October 2021 - March
2022
Nearest Station: South Kensington

Internationally renowned photographer
Sebastião Salgado presents a series of
breathtaking photographs that celebrate the
indigenous peoples and varied landscapes of
the Brazilian rainforest. For six years, Salgado
worked with twelve different indigenous
communities to create over 200 powerful
black-and-white photographs that uncover
his vision of the Amazon when the forest is
approaching a crucial tipping point in the fight
against climate change. The exhibition contains
nudity and content that some visitors might
find challenging.
www.sciencemuseum.org.uk

We Are History
Somerset House; 14 October 2021 – 6
February 2022
Nearest Station: Temple

A group exhibition exploring the relationship
between human impact on nature and legacies
of colonialism showcasing works from nine
artists with personal connections to countries
in the Caribbean, South America and Africa.
Featuring photography, print, textile and
video works, it seeks to expand the common
narrative around climate change, bringing to the
fore the perspectives of the communities who
often feel the impact of the climate crisis the
most keenly, yet least visibly on the world stage
today.
www.somersethouse.org.uk

**Fighting Talk: One Man's Journey
From Abandonment to Trafalgar**
Foundling Museum; 15 October 2021– 27
February 2022
Nearest Station: Russell Square

A first-hand account of The Battle of Trafalgar is

revealed through the lens of the extraordinary autobiography of eighteenth-century working-class boy George King (1787– 1857). The exhibition explores the origins of the Foundling Hospital – the UK's first children's charity – and the contribution it made to Britain's military and workforce in the 1700s. Discover King's story as he describes being press-ganged into the Navy, surviving brutal battles that left him traumatised, meeting enslaved people in South Carolina and letting his hair down at the theatre in London's West End.
foundlingmuseum.org.uk

Zadok Ben-David: Natural Reserve

Shirley Sherwood Gallery of Botanical Art, Kew Gardens; 16 October 2021 – 27 March 2022
Nearest Station: Kew Gardens

This is the first solo exhibition in the UK of the internationally renowned artist and sculptor to incorporate new and existing works since 2008. It centres on themes of tragedy and hope, focusing on the constantly evolving relationship between humanity and the natural world.
www.kew.org

Natural History Museum Ice Rink

Natural History Museum; 22 October 2021 – 16 January 2022
Nearest Station: South Kensington

Skate in the front garden of this magnificent Victorian building. After an incredible 16 years, this is the final year for the ice rink. The Museum is transforming its five-acre gardens into a hub for urban wildlife, as part of a national campaign to encourage people to help nature on their doorsteps.
www.nhm.ac.uk

London: Port City

Museum of London Docklands; 22 October 2021 – 8 May 2022
Nearest Station: West India Quay (DLR)

A well-chosen location as the Museum of London Docklands building was originally part of West India Docks, London's first enclosed dock system. Valuable cargoes from around the world were unloaded here from 1802 until its closure in 1980. The exhibition reveals the ongoing impact of the Port of London on our capital city, its people, design, culture, prosperity and global position through 200 years of extraordinary experiences.
www.museumoflondon.org.uk

Waste Age

Design Museum; 23 October 2021 – 20 February 2022
Nearest Station: High Street Kensington

We live in an age defined by our waste. Design has helped create this problem and it will be crucial in solving it. Discover how our production of waste has escalated since the mid-twentieth century and face the epic scale of this man-made crisis through immersive installations. Then explore how what we throw away can be transformed into new resources, and how design can help usher in a new age where there is no such thing as waste.
designmuseum.org

Light Lines: The Architectural Photographs of Hélène Binet

Royal Academy; 23 October 2021 – 23 January 2022
Nearest Station: Piccadilly Circus

Rediscover the power and presence of architectural wonders by Le Corbusier, Zaha Hadid RA and others through Hélène Binet's photographic lens. Considered "the architect's photographer" by many, this intimate exhibition of around 90 photographs spans projects from across Binet's career.
www.royalacademy.org.uk

Late Constable

Royal Academy; 30 October 2021 – 13
February 2022
Nearest Station: Piccadilly Circus

This is the first survey of the late work of
John Constable (1776–1837). It explores the
last twelve years of the artist's career, from
1825 until his unexpected death in 1837.
Characterised by the expressive brushwork
that came to define Constable's late career,
the exhibition brings together over 50 works
including paintings and oil sketches as well as
watercolours, drawings and prints, taking an
in-depth look at the development of the artist's
late style.
www.royalacademy.org.uk

Winter at Southbank Centre

South Bank; November 2021 – January 2022
Nearest Station: Waterloo

Enjoy a packed programme of free and ticketed
events and activities, as Southbank Centre
transforms the south bank of the Thames into
a festive wonderland for its annual Winter
festival including a Christmas market and family
activities.
www.southbankcentre.co.uk

Hogarth and Europe

Tate Britain; 3 November 2021 – 20 March
2022
Nearest Station: Pimlico

Few artists have defined an era as much as
William Hogarth (1697–1764), whose vivid,
satirical depictions of eighteenth-century
England continue to capture the imagination
today. This major exhibition presents his work
in a fresh light, seen for the first time alongside
works by his continental contemporaries.
It explores the parallels and exchanges that
crossed borders and the cosmopolitan
character of Hogarth's art.
www.tate.org.uk

Peru: A Journey in Time

British Museum; 11 November 2021 – 20 February 2022
Nearest Station: Tottenham Court Road

Marking Peru's bicentennial year of independence, this exhibition highlights the history, beliefs and cultural achievements of the different peoples who lived here from around 2500 BC to the arrival of Europeans in the 1500s, and their legacy in the centuries that followed. Discover how people have thrived for millennia in one of the most complex and challenging environments on the planet.
www.britishmuseum.org

Moulin Rouge! The Musical

Piccadilly Theatre; 12 November 2021 – 9 April 2022
Nearest Station: Piccadilly Circus

Step into the famous Parisian nightclub with this musical based on the blockbuster 2001 film. Playing for the first time in the heart of the West End, the enchanting story features a vibrant mix of new songs and old favourites.
www.thepiccadillytheatre.com

Hogwarts in the Snow

Warner Bros Studio Tour; 13 November 2021 – 16 January 2022
Nearest Station: Watford Junction

Lined with Christmas trees, the Great Hall has a festive makeover with the long tables laden with a mouth-watering Christmas feast. A blanket of filmmaking snow covers the majestic Hogwarts castle model and shop fronts of Diagon Alley as part of the wintery transformation.
www.wbstudiotour.co.uk

The Book of Mormon

Prince of Wales Theatre; 15 November 2021 – 2 April 2022
Nearest Station: Piccadilly Circus

A satirical musical telling the story of two young Mormon missionaries as they naively try to convert the locals, who are more worried about war, famine, poverty and AIDS than religion.
thebookofmormonmusical.com

Ancient Greeks: Science and Wisdom

Science Museum; 17 November 2021 – 5 June 2022
Nearest Station: South Kensington

Curiosity and investigation are central to furthering our understanding of the universe today. Ancient Greek thinkers shared a similar philosophy. Step back through millennia in this free exhibition and discover how this ancient civilization questioned, contemplated, and debated the natural world.
www.sciencemuseum.org.uk

Fabergé in London: Romance to Revolution

V&A; 20 November 2021 – 8 May 2022
Nearest Station: South Kensington

The exhibition explores master goldsmith, Carl Fabergé – whose internationally recognised firm symbolised Russian craftsmanship, luxury and elegance – and the Anglo-Russian relationship which saw the opening of a London branch in 1903.
vam.ac.uk

Durer's Journey's: Travels of a Renaissance Artist

National Gallery; 20 November 2021 – 27 February 2022
Nearest Station: Charing Cross

This is the first major UK exhibition of German Renaissance artist Albrecht Dürer in nearly 20 years. Through paintings, drawings, prints, and letters, this exhibition follows Dürer's travels

across Europe, bringing to life the artist himself, and the people and places he visited.
www.nationalgallery.org.uk

Lubaina Himid

Tate Modern; 25 November 2021 – 3 July 2022
Nearest Station: Southwark

This theatrical exhibition by the Turner Prize-winning artist includes recent work alongside highlights from across her influential career, often exploring overlooked and invisible aspects of social history and contemporary life. Taking inspiration from her interest in theatre, the exhibition unfolds in a sequence of scenes designed to place visitors centre-stage and backstage.
www.tate.org.uk

Amy: Beyond The Stage

Design Museum; 26 November 2021 – 10 April 2022
Nearest Station: High Street Kensington

Discover the story of Amy's early career through her recordings and teenage notebooks to unravel the creative process behind her music, and pay tribute to her rich range of influences, from Dinah Washington to Mark Ronson, Camden to '60s pop, Motown to jazz.
designmuseum.org

Life Between Islands: Caribbean-British Art 50s – Now

Tate Britain; 1 December 2021 – 3 April 2022
Nearest Station: Pimlico

A landmark group exhibition spanning a whole ocean and half a century, this exhibition explores work by artists from the Caribbean who made their home in Britain, alongside other British artists who have also made work addressing Caribbean themes and heritage. It celebrates how people from the Caribbean have forged new communities and identities in post-war Britain – and in doing so have transformed British culture and society.
www.tate.org.uk

Animal Therapy: the Cats of Louis Wain

Bethlem Museum of the Mind; 4 December 2021 – April 2022 (tbc)
Nearest Station: East Croydon

Focusing on the cat drawings of Louis Wain (1860–1939) that featured anthropomorphized large-eyed felines, this exhibition coincides with a new film about Wain starring Benedict Cumberbatch. 'The Electrical Life of Louis Wain' depicts him as a loveable, inspirational hero with a courageous and infectious spirit, who saw the world in a unique and delightful way throughout his long life full of adventure, inspiring people to do the same. Later in life, he was confined to mental institutions and was alleged to have suffered from schizophrenia.
museumofthemind.org.uk

Kehinde Wiley

National Gallery; 10 December 2021 – 18 April 2022
Nearest Station: Charing Cross

The work of American artist Wiley makes reference to the canon of European portraiture by positioning contemporary black sitters, from a range of ethnic and social backgrounds, in the poses of the original historical, religious or mythological figures. In this exhibition, Wiley shifts his focus to another European tradition, landscape painting. Through new artworks, including film and painting, he looks at European Romanticism and its focus on epic scenes of oceans and mountains, building relationships with the gallery's collection of historical landscapes and seascapes by Turner, Claude, Vernet and Friedrich.
www.nationalgallery.org.uk

JANUARY 2022

Cirque du Soleil – LUZIA
Royal Albert Hall; 12 January – 12 February 2021
Nearest Station: High Street Kensington

Escape to an imaginary Mexico – a sumptuous world suspended between dreams and reality in this European premiere of LUZIA. Smoothly passing from an old movie set to the ocean to a smoky dance hall or an arid desert, the show cleverly brings to the stage multiple places, faces and sounds of Mexico taken from both tradition and modernity. The arrival of LUZIA marks 30 years since Cirque du Soleil first brought its captivating magic and awe-inspiring acrobatics to the UK.
www.royalalberthall.com

Raymondo
London Coliseum; 13 – 23 January 2022
Nearest Station: Charing Cross

Set in England in 1854, Raymonda runs away from her comfortable life to become a nurse in the Crimean War. There, she becomes engaged to a soldier, John, but soon develops feelings for his friend Abdur, a leader of the Ottoman army. As turmoil grows around and inside her, who will she give her heart to? This is an English National Ballet world premiere before it goes on a national tour. The show takes inspiration from the groundbreaking spirit of Florence Nightingale and the women who supported the war effort in Crimea.
www.ballet.org.uk

Hamlet
Sam Wanamaker Playhouse; 21 January – 9 April 2022
Nearest Station: Southwark

Performed for the first time by candlelight in the intimate confines of the Shakespeare Globe's Sam Wanamaker Playhouse. The low lighting intensifies this tale of corruption and disruption to life. This production of Hamlet takes you inside the mind of the grief-stricken prince as Hamlet seeks revenge for his father's alleged murder.
www.shakespearesglobe.com

Gainsborough's Blue Boy
National Gallery; 22 January – 15 May 2022
Nearest Station: Charing Cross

'The Blue Boy' represents the best of eighteenth-century British art. In the winter of 1922, Gainsborough's 'The Blue Boy' hung at the National Gallery for three weeks before it sailed across the Atlantic to its new home in California. It was a public farewell to a beloved painting. 100 years later (to the day), Gainsborough's masterpiece is returning. This is the first time the painting has been loaned by The Huntington – it is a once-in-a-century opportunity to see this iconic work in the UK.
nationalgallery.org.uk

A Number
The Old Vic; 24 January – 19 March 2022
Nearest Station: Waterloo

Lennie James and Paapa Essiedu play father and sons in Caryl Churchill's gripping drama about what it costs to start again. Every parent makes mistakes. Salter makes a number of them. Now 35 years later, his only child realises he's not alone.
www.oldvictheatre.com

Francis Bacon: Man and Beast
Royal Academy; 29 January – 17 April 2022
Nearest Station: Piccadilly Circus

Francis Bacon (1909–1992) is recognised as one of the most important artists of the twentieth century. Since his death, the world has changed in ways that make his unnerving work ever more prescient. This is the first exhibition to chart the development of the artist's work through his fascination with animals, and how this impacted his treatment of his ultimate subject: the human figure. It includes around 45 paintings spanning his career from the 1930s through to the final painting he ever made in 1991, which is being exhibited publicly for the first time in the UK. Among the works, a trio of paintings of bullfights, all made in 1969, is also on display together for the first time. www.royalacademy.org.uk

MORE JANUARY 2022 EVENTS

- New Year's Day Parade: 1 Jan (Marching bands, cheerleaders and huge inflatables through the streets of central London)
- Twelfth Night: Sunday close to 5 Jan (Annual free celebration mixing ancient Midwinter seasonal customs and contemporary festivity on Bankside)
- Canary Wharf Winter Lights: Jan tbc (Light installations and interactive art around Canary Wharf)
- London Short Film Festival: 14–23 Jan (Watch short film screenings from emerging filmmakers)
- London Art Fair: 19–23 Jan (Annual fair that brings together more than 100 galleries to showcase museum-quality contemporary artworks from the early twentieth century to today's leading artists)

FEBRUARY 2022

The Merchant of Venice
Sam Wanamaker Playhouse, 18 February – 9 April 2022
Nearest Station: Southwark

Abigail Graham makes her Shakespeare's Globe directorial debut with Shakespeare's complex exploration of prejudice, patriarchy and capitalism. This production exposes the fault lines of a society built on religious and moral hypocrisy and brings together the personal and political in a re-imagining of Shylock's play. www.shakespearesglobe.com

Whistler's Woman in White: Joanna Hiffernan
Royal Academy; 26 February – 22 May 2022
Nearest Station: Piccadilly Circus

This is the first exhibition to shine a light on the critical role that Hiffernan played in establishing Whistler's reputation as one of the most influential artists of the late nineteenth century. Consisting of around seventy works, including innovative paintings, drawings and prints, it offers a comprehensive account of Hiffernan's role as an active participant in Whistler's creative and personal life for more than twenty years. The exhibition also explores the works of Gustave Courbet, who painted Hiffernan when she and Whistler joined Courbet one summer in Normandy, as well as Whistler's relationship with the Pre-Raphaelites and the influence of Japonisme on his works. Whistler and Hiffernan's legacy is revealed through a final chorus of "woman in white" paintings by artists such as John Everett Millais and Gustav Klimt. www.royalacademy.org.uk

Legacies: Caribbean Recruitment (working title)
London Transport Museum; opening February 2022

Nearest Station: Covent Garden

Explore how Caribbean transport workers have shaped the capital when London Transport recruited from the Caribbean in the 1950s to 1970s. By working on the Tube, buses and in all areas of public transport, these intrepid young men and women who started new lives in London have exerted an enduring influence.
www.ltmuseum.co.uk

Henry V

Donmar Warehouse; 11 February – 9 April 2022
Nearest Station: Leicester Square

Shakespeare's ever-popular play is a thrilling study of nationalism, war and the psychology of power. Kit Harington leads the cast in an exciting modern production directed by Donmar Associate Director Max Webster, exploring what it means to be English and our relationship to Europe, asking: do we ever get the leaders we deserve?
www.donmarwarehouse.com

Beatrix Potter: Drawn to Nature

V&A; 12 February – 25 September 2022
Nearest Station: South Kensington

The V&A has joined forces with the National Trust to celebrate the life and work of one of the best-loved children's authors of the twentieth century. Using playful staging and immersive design, it showcases original watercolours, drawings and manuscripts as well as personal artefacts including letters, photographs, furniture and decorative art. It takes visitors of all ages on a journey to discover Potter's extraordinary and multifaceted life as a natural scientist, farmer and conservationist in the Lake District, bringing to light the places, people and animals that inspired some of Potter's most beloved characters, from Jemima Puddle-duck to

Benjamin Bunny and Peter Rabbit.
www.vam.ac.uk

Surrealism Beyond Borders
Tate Modern; 24 February – 29 August 2022
Nearest Station: Southwark

This landmark exhibition expands the story of surrealism and reveals how artists around the world – from Tokyo to Mexico City, Cairo to Paris, and Martinique to Bucharest – were united by the movement's subversive ideas and revolutionary spirit.
www.tate.org.uk

Shen Yun
Eventim Apollo; 26 February – 6 March 2022
Nearest Station: Hammersmith

An epic production that takes you on a journey through 5,000 years of Chinese civilisation featuring classical Chinese dance. Enter a world where maidens danced with ethereal grace and warriors trained with explosive vigour. Where timeless tales of valour, virtue, and humour were born. Where scholars and artists sought harmony with the Tao, or the 'Way' of the universe, and where heaven and earth connected to inspire hope for humanity.
www.shenyunperformingarts.org

MORE FEBRUARY 2022 EVENTS

- Chinese New Year celebrations: 7 Feb tbc (Parade along Shaftesbury Avenue and Charing Cross Road with free entertainment in Trafalgar Square)
- Strictly Come Dancing (O2 Arena): 11–13 Feb (Celebs and professional dancers from the BBC One TV series)

MARCH 2022

Kyōsai: The Israel Goldman Collection
Royal Academy; 19 March – 19 June 2022
Nearest Station: Piccadilly Circus

Kawanabe Kyōsai (1831–1889) was the
most exciting and popular Japanese painter of
the late nineteenth century. A child prodigy
and draughtsman of the highest ability, his
art is humorous, provocative, energetic and
outrageous. The exhibition focuses largely
on the art of sekiga, 'spontaneous paintings',
produced at 'calligraphy and painting parties'
(shogakai) which were often fuelled by
prodigious amounts of saké.
www.royalacademy.org.uk

**Fashioning Masculinities: The Art of
Menswear**
V&A; 19 March – 6 November 2022
Nearest Station: South Kensington

At a moment of unprecedented creativity in
men's fashion and reflection on gender, this
exhibition explores how designers, tailors and
artists – and their clients and sitters – have
constructed and performed masculinity, and
unpicked it at the seams. It's the V&A's first
major exhibition focusing on menswear and
aims to celebrate the power, artistry and
diversity of masculine attire and appearance.
www.vam.ac.uk

Tate Britain Commission: Hew Locke
Tate Britain; 22 March - 23 October 2022
Nearest Station: Pimlico

Hew Locke is creating a new work for the
iconic Duveen Galleries at the heart of the
building. The Duveen Galleries were the first
public galleries in England designed specifically
for the display of sculpture. Every year a British
artist is invited to make new work in response
to the grand space and to Tate's collection. Hew
Locke was born in Edinburgh in 1959, he then

spent his formative years living in Georgetown, Guyana from 1966 to 1980. He obtained an MA in Sculpture from the Royal College of Art, London in 1994.
www.tate.org.uk

To Kill A Mockingbird

Gielgud Theatre; 31 March 2021 – 13 August 2022
Nearest Station: Leicester Square

This is a Broadway transfer following a hugely successful run. It has been adapted by Aaron Sorkin but is based on Harper Lee's Pulitzer-winning novel. The play tells the story of young Scout and her father Atticus Finch, a lawyer tasked with defending a local, Tom Robinson, who is accused of rape. The novel explores justice and racial tension in a small Southern town and is one of the best-selling novels of all time.
www.delfontmackintosh.co.uk

MORE MARCH 2022 EVENTS

- Pancake Day Races: 1 March (Shrove Tuesday pancake-flipping races across the city)
- St Patrick's Day Parade: Sunday 20 March tbc (Parade followed by performances in Trafalgar Square)
- Mother's Day: Sunday 27 March (While Mothering Sunday is in May for much of the world, in the UK we celebrate in March)
- London Games Festival: date tbc (One of the world's biggest games festivals)

APRIL 2022

Japan: Courts and Culture

Queen's Gallery, Buckingham Palace; 8 April 2022 – 5 February 2023
Nearest Station: Victoria

The Royal Collection contains one of the finest holdings of Japanese works of art in the western world, significant for both the unique provenance and exceptional quality of the objects. For the first time, highlights from the collection have been brought to tell the story of the diplomatic, artistic and cultural exchanges between Britain and Japan from the reigns of James I to Queen Elizabeth II. Including rare examples of porcelain, lacquer, armour and embroidered screens, the exhibition offers a unique insight into the relationship between the imperial and royal courts over a period of 300 years.
www.rct.uk

Football: Designing the Beautiful Game

Design Museum; 8 April – 29 August 2022
Nearest Station: High Street Kensington

It is estimated that more than half the population of the planet – some 3.5 billion people – watched part of the FIFA World Cup in 2018. Football is unquestionably the world's most popular sport, with a dedicated fan base and truly international reach, its diversity and passion touching the lives of people from all walks of life. This exhibition unpicks how design has pushed the game to its technical and emotional limits. From the master-planning of the world's most significant football stadiums to the innovative materials used in today's boots, the graphic design of team badges and the grassroots initiatives pushing back against the sport's commercialisation. Glimpse a rare insight into the designers and creative processes that have made football what it is

today.
designmuseum.org

Raphael
National Gallery; 9 April – 31 July 2022
Nearest Station: Charing Cross

Originally scheduled for October 2020, in the
year that marked the 500th anniversary of
Raphael's death, the exhibition is the first to
explore the complete career of this giant of the
Italian Renaissance. It looks at his celebrated
paintings and drawings as well as his work in
architecture, poetry, and design for sculpture,
tapestry and prints.
www.nationalgallery.org.uk

Marys Seacole
Donmar Warehouse; 15 April – 4 June 2022
Nearest Station: Leicester Square

Mary Seacole was the pioneering Jamaican
nurse who bravely voyaged to heal soldiers in
the Crimean War. She was a traveller, a hotelier
and a businesswoman. Putting the concept of a
biopic through a kaleidoscope, the production
is a dazzling exploration, across oceans and
eras, of what it means to be a woman who is
paid to care, and how, ultimately, no one is in
charge of their own story.
www.donmarwarehouse.com

Into The Woods
The Old Vic; 16 April – 9 July 2022
Nearest Station: Waterloo

A revival of Stephen Sondheim and James
Lapine's production co-directed by Terry
Gillam. It combines fairytale characters into an
original story of a baker and his wife who try
to reverse the curse put upon them by a witch.
Relying on help from Cinderella, Little Red
Riding Hood, Rapunzel and Jack, they venture
into the woods to have their wishes granted.
www.oldvictheatre.com

Walter Sickert
Tate Britain; 28 April – 18 September 2022
Nearest Station: Pimlico

Walter Sickert's evocative paintings of life in the late nineteenth and early twentieth centuries explore his radically modern compositions, pioneering use of photography and fascination with the media, the stage and the rise of celebrity.
www.tate.org.uk

MORE APRIL 2022 EVENTS

- The Boat Race: date tbc (Annual contest between two rowing crews from Oxford and Cambridge universities)
- The Passion of Jesus in Trafalgar Square: 15 April (Free, full-scale re-enactment of Jesus's final days, from his arrest to his resurrection)
- Easter Sunday: 17 April
- Queen's birthday: 21 April (This is her 'real' birthday and not the public one we celebrate in June)
- Feast of St George: 21 April tbc (Trafalgar Square festival for England's national day)
- Vaisakhi Festival in Trafalgar Square: date tbc (Sikh festival with free performances)
- Houses of Parliament Guided Tours (During Parliamentary Easter recess)

MAY 2022

Weird Sensation Feels Good
Design Museum; Opens 13 May 2022
Nearest Station: High Street Kensington

Have you ever heard a sound that has brought you a sense of calm? Or even made your skin tingle? Millions around the world are part of an online community who experience ASMR (Autonomous Sensory Meridian Response): a physical sensation of euphoria or deep calm, sometimes a tingling in the body, triggered through sound, touch, and movement. This is the first exhibition of its kind to lift the world of ASMR out from your screen and into physical space. Step into an acoustically tuned environment and understand how people are creating sensory responses using new and existing tools and materials.
designmuseum.org

FA Cup Final
Wembley Stadium; Saturday 14 May 2022
Nearest Station: Wembley Park

The 2021–22 season is the 150th anniversary of the FA Cup competition. A total of 729 clubs have entered the oldest football tournament in the world for this season and by May 2022 it will be down to two teams deciding who lifts the trophy. The winners qualify for the 2022–23 UEFA Europa League group stage.
www.thefa.com

Cornelia Parker
Tate Britain; 19 May – 16 October 2022
Nearest Station: Pimlico

Cornelia Parker, one of Britain's most celebrated contemporary artists, is the subject of this career-spanning survey. The exhibition features many of her mesmerising installations and reveals her formally innovative and socially engaged approach to sculpture, film,

photography, drawing and embroidery.
www.tate.org.uk

ABBA Voyage

ABBA Arena; 27 May 2022 - 27 May 2025
Nearest Station: Stratford

ABBA Voyage is the long-awaited concert from
one of the biggest pop acts of all time. See
ABBA's avatars accompanied by a 10-piece
live band, in a custom-built arena at Queen
Elizabeth Olympic Park.
abbavoyage.com

MORE MAY 2022 EVENTS

- Remembering The Oscars: 2–7 May
  (Celebrate Oscar-winning songs at the
  Peacock Theatre)
- Regent's Park Open Air Theatre: May–
  Sept (Cultural hub in the beautiful
  surroundings of a Royal Park)
- Eid Festival: May tbc (Celebration of
  Muslim culture in Trafalgar Square)
- RHS Chelsea Flower Show: 24–28 May
  2022 (Annual prestigious flower show)

JUNE 2022

Picasso Ingres: Face to Face
National Gallery; 3 June – 9 October 2022
Nearest Station: Charing Cross

For the first time ever a painting by Pablo
Picasso (Woman with a Book, 1932) from the
Norton Simon Museum in Pasadena, California,
and the painting by Jean-Auguste-Dominique
Ingres (Madame Moitessier, 1856) which
famously inspired it, are on shown side by side
as part of a special collaboration between the
two institutions. Picasso admired Ingres and
referred to him throughout his career. Picasso's
affinity with Ingres can clearly be demonstrated
not only in painting but also extensively in his
drawings and studies during his neoclassical
phase in the 1920s.
www.nationalgallery.org.uk

The Car Man
Royal Albert Hall; 9–19 June 2022
Nearest Station: High Street Kensington

Matthew Bourne's spectacular re-imagining
of 'The Car Man' was originally scheduled
to run in June 2021 as a centrepiece of
the Royal Albert Hall's 150th-anniversary
celebrations. A dance-thriller based
on Bizet's beloved 'Carmen',' The Car
Man' has been completely reimagined for the
gladiatorial arena of the Royal Albert Hall,
with an expanded company of 65 dancers
and musicians, and a live orchestra. A frisson
of danger is added as the dancers perform
throughout the auditorium.
www.royalalberthall.com

Grace Jones' Meltdown
Southbank Centre; 10–19 June 2022
Nearest Station: Waterloo

Grace Jones is the curator of this annual
Southbank Centre festival and has chosen acts
including Solange, Peaches, The Love Unlimited
Synth Orchestra and Skunk Anansie. This is the
27th edition of the UK's longest-running artist-
curated music festival.
www.southbankcentre.co.uk

Africa Fashion
V&A; 11 June 2022 – 16 April 2023
Nearest Station: South Kensington

A major exhibition celebrating the irresistible
creativity, ingenuity and unstoppable global
impact of contemporary African fashion
creatives. Over 250 objects spanning iconic
mid-twentieth century designers to the present
day, complemented by photographs and textiles
from the V&A's collections, explores the vitality
and innovation of a fashion scene as dynamic
and varied as the continent itself.
www.vam.ac.uk

Summer Exhibition 2022
Royal Academy; 21 June – 21 August 2022
Nearest Station: Piccadilly Circus

The world's largest open submission
contemporary art show is now in its 254th
year. It provides a unique platform for emerging
and established artists to showcase their works
to an international audience, comprising a
range of media from painting, printmaking and
photography, to sculpture, architecture and film.
It has been held each year without interruption
since 1769. Around 1200 works go on display,
the majority of which are for sale offering
visitors an opportunity to purchase original
work. Funds raised support the exhibiting
artists, the postgraduate students studying in
the RA Schools and the work of the Royal
Academy.
www.royalacademy.org.uk

Wimbledon Lawn Tennis Championships
The All England Lawn Tennis Club; 27 June – 10 July 2022
Nearest Station: Southfields

Every summer this corner of southwest London hosts the longest-running tennis tournament in the world, and one of four annual Grand Slam tennis events held around the globe. Games are still played on the original playing surface, grass, and there's a strict white-only dress code for players.
www.wimbledon.com

MORE JUNE 2022 EVENTS

- Trooping the Colour: 2 June (Queen's official birthday parade)
- Open Garden Squares Weekend: 11–12 June (Interesting green spaces across London are unlocked for one weekend only)
- London Fashion Week: date tbc (Designer catwalks, expert talks and pop-up shops at this industry event open to the public)

JULY 2022

Milton Avery: American Colourist
Royal Academy; 15 July – 16 October 2022
Nearest Station: Piccadilly Circus

Milton Avery (1885–1965) has long been recognised in the United States as one of the most important and influential twentieth-century American artists. Avery's compositions, taken from daily life, including portraits and landscapes, are imbued with a colour sensibility, harmony and balance which was to have a major influence on the next artistic generation. Avery played a vital role in the development of Abstract Expressionism, through his close association with some of the younger exponents of the movement, such as Mark Rothko, Barnett Newman and Adolph Gottlieb. His work defies distinct categorisation, falling between the time of the American Impressionists and the Abstract Expressionists, both of which had a significant impact on his oeuvre. Avery was famously prolific, and this survey features around seventy of his most celebrated paintings from the early 1930s to the 1960s. The last retrospective of his work was held at the Whitney Museum of American Art in 1982 and this is the first solo exhibition of Milton Avery in Europe.
www.royalacademy.org.uk

Sister Act
Hammersmith Apollo; 19 July – 28 August 2022
Nearest Station: Hammersmith

Initially booked for 2020, then rescheduled to 2021 and rescheduled again, Whoopi Goldberg is starring in Sister Act reprising her lead role from the hit 1992 film. Goldberg plays disco diva Deloris Van Cartier who ends up in protective custody in a convent, overseen by the Mother Superior, played here by Jennifer Saunders.
www.eventimapollo.com

MORE JULY 2022 EVENTS

- RHS Hampton Court Palace Garden Festival: 4–10 July (World's biggest flower show with beautiful horticultural displays)
- The Proms: Jul–Sept (Annual 8-week summer season of classical concerts)
- Summer Opening of Buckingham Palace: July–Sept (Visit the State Rooms while the Queen is away)
- UEFA Women's EURO 2022: 6–31 July (England host the football tournament with the final taking place at London's Wembley Stadium)
- Cirque du Soleil – Corteo: 13–17 July (O2 Arena)
- Taste of London: date tbc (Join London's top restaurants and celebrity chefs for the ultimate alfresco feast in Regent's Park)

AUGUST 2022

Kids Week

London theatres; 1–31 August 2022

Every year, for the whole of August, a child aged 16 or under can go to any participating theatre show for free where tickets are available as long as they are accompanied by a full paying adult. Adults can also buy up to two extra children's tickets at half price and there are no booking fees.
officiallondontheatre.com/kids-week

Notting Hill Carnival

Notting Hill; 28 & 29 August 2022
Nearest Stations: Ladbroke Grove/Notting Hill *Gate/Westbourne Park*

Europe's largest street party comes to west London every summer for the August Bank Holiday weekend. Sunday is Children's Day

and Monday is the Grand Parade. Expect lots of mobile sound systems as the party goes on after the parade passes.
www.thelondonnottinghillcarnival.com

MORE AUGUST 2022 EVENTS

- Greenwich+Docklands International Festival: Aug–Sept (One of London's largest free outdoor arts festivals)
- Film4 Summer Screen at Somerset House: dates tbc (Two weeks of open-air cinema)
- The Osmonds: A New Musical: 23–27 Aug (New musical at New Wimbledon Theatre of one of the world's biggest ever boybands)
- Houses of Parliament Guided Tours (During Parliamentary Summer recess)

SEPTEMBER 2022

William Kentridge

Royal Academy; 24 September – 11 December 2022
Nearest Station: Piccadilly Circus

Working closely with the internationally celebrated South African artist and his studio, this ambitious exhibition has been specifically curated for the Royal Academy and shows the broad repertoire of Kentridge's extraordinary forty-year career. It brings together rarely seen works from the 1980s through to the present day, including the first UK presentation of a new animated film shown in an immersive setting, and a site-specific wall drawing created in the galleries.
www.royalacademy.org.uk

Hallyu! The Korean Wave

V&A; 24 September 2022 – 25 June 2023

Nearest Station: South Kensington

Showcasing the colourful and dynamic popular culture of South Korea, exploring the makings of the Korean Wave and its global impact on the creative industries of cinema, drama, music, fandom, beauty and fashion. Rising to prominence in the late 1990s, the first tides of hallyu, meaning 'Korean Wave', rippled across Asia before becoming a worldwide phenomenon that challenges the currents of global pop culture today.
www.vam.ac.uk

MORE SEPTEMBER 2022 EVENTS

- BBC Proms in the Park: mid-Sept (Open-air classical concert in Hyde Park on the closing night of the two-month classical music festival)
- Totally Thames: 1–30 Sept (Month-long season of arts, cultural and river events throughout the 42-mile stretch of the Thames in London)
- Open House London: dates tbc: (World's largest architectural festival)
- Laver Cup: 23–25 September (Tennis tournament at The O2 played on a black court)

OCTOBER 2022

Lucian Freud New Perspectives
National Gallery; 1 October 2022 – 22 January 2023
Nearest Station: Charing Cross

The exhibition presents the paintings of one of Britain's most notorious figurative painters, Lucian Freud (1922–2011). It spans a lifetime of work, showing how Freud's painting changed during 70 years of practice from his early and intimate works to his well-known, large-scale canvases and his monumental naked portraits. This is the first major survey of his paintings for 10 years.
www.nationalgallery.org.uk

London Marathon
Sunday 2 October 2022

This is the third successive year that the London Marathon is being held in October rather than its traditional April date. See up to 50,000 runners on the 26.2 mile-course from Greenwich to The Mall.
www.virginmoneylondonmarathon.com

Cezanne
Tate Modern; 6 October 2022 – 26 February 2023
Nearest Station: Southwark

A fresh take on this pivotal figure in modern art. Featuring his portraits, landscapes and still lifes, and including many paintings never shown in the UK before, this exhibition explores the ambitions, innovations and contradictions that defined Cezanne's life and work.
www.tate.org.uk

Objects of Desire: Surrealism and Design 1924 – Today
Design Museum; Opens 14 October 2022
Nearest Station: High Street Kensington

One of the most influential art movements of the twentieth century, Surrealism combined and reinvented everyday objects to create dreamlike imagery. The results include iconic works of art such as Marcel Duchamp's Bicycle Wheel (1913) and Salvador Dali's Lobster Telephone (1936). This is the first exhibition to examine the previously unexplored influence that Surrealism has had on design over the past 100 years, from furniture and interiors to graphic design, fashion and photography. It brings together classic works of art and design as well contemporary responses from around the globe.
designmuseum.org

MORE OCTOBER 2022 EVENTS

- Hyundai Commission: October 2022 – April 2023: (Annual site-specific installation by a contemporary artist in Tate Modern's iconic Turbine Hall)
- Camden Oktoberfest: four Saturdays in October (Celebration of the famous Bavarian beer festival)

NOVEMBER 2022

Irma Boom
Design Museum; November 2022 – Spring 2023
Nearest Station: High Street Kensington

Irma Boom is one of the most prolific book designers working today. With more than 380 books to her name, the Dutch designer is renowned for the way she challenges the format to make each volume a unique experience. This retrospective exhibition gets inside her craft, revealing not just her creative process but the power of the book itself. With this exhibition, Boom has set herself the challenge of finding novel ways to tell the story of her practice. It features her collaborations with Rem Koolhaas, Sheila Hicks, Chanel and many others, and brings to light the work of a master designer, even if she likes to call herself simply a "book maker".
designmuseum.org

Making Modernism
Royal Academy; 12 November 2022 – 12 February 2023
Nearest Station: Piccadilly Circus

This is the first major UK exhibition devoted to women artists working in Germany in the early twentieth century. It includes 65 paintings and works on paper primarily by Paula Modersohn-Becker, Käthe Kollwitz, Gabriele Münter and Marianne Werefkin, with additional works by Erma Bossi and Jacoba van Heemskerck; most of these artworks have never been exhibited in this country before. Although less familiar than their male counterparts, these artists were central to the development and dissemination of modernism. Seen through the lens of its female practitioners, key themes of modernism such as self-portraiture, still-life and urban and rural scenes are re-evaluated, and attention is focussed on the female body, childhood and maternal experience.

www.royalacademy.org.uk

Magdalena Abakanowicz
Tate Modern, 17 November 2022 – 21 May 2023
Nearest Station: Southwark

In the 1960s and 70s, this Polish artist created radical sculptures from woven fibre. They were soft not hard; ambiguous and organic; towering works that hung from the ceiling and pioneered a new form of installation. They became known as the Abakans. This exhibition presents a rare opportunity to explore this extraordinary body of work. Many of the most significant Abakans have been brought together in a forest-like display in the 64-metre long gallery space of the Blavatnik Building at Tate Modern.
www.tate.org.uk

Lynette Yiadom-Boakye: Fly In League With The Night
Tate Britain; 24 November 2022 – 26 February 2023
Nearest Station: Pimlico

This acclaimed exhibition was cut short in 2020 so is returning to show the British artist's enigmatic paintings of fictitious people. It brings together around 70 works from 2003 to the present day in the most extensive survey of the artist's career to date. The figures in her paintings are created from found images and her imagination. Both familiar and mysterious, they invite viewers to project their own interpretations and raise important questions of identity and representation.
www.tate.org.uk

MORE NOVEMBER 2022 EVENTS

- Lord Mayor's Show: date tbc (Newly-elected Lord Mayor of the City of London travels through the streets to swear loyalty to the Crown)
- Pantomime season: Nov–Dec (See

female 'lead boys' and male 'dames' in festive family theatre shows)
- Winter Wonderland: Nov–Jan (Festive fun in Hyde Park with fairground rides, shows, shopping, etc)
- Christmas at Kew: Nov–Jan (After-dark festivities with stunning illuminations)
- Hogwarts in the Snow: Nov–Feb (Warner Bros Studio Tour's annual festive makeover)

DECEMBER 2022

Trafalgar Square Christmas Tree Lighting

Trafalgar Square; 1 December 2022
Nearest Station: Charing Cross

While the Christmas lights go on across London during November, on the first Thursday in December there's a small ceremony to switch on the lights on the Trafalgar Square Christmas tree. There is then carol singing around the tree most nights before Christmas Day.
www.london.gov.uk/events

Nutcracker Ballet

London Coliseum; December 2022 – January 2023
Nearest Station: Leicester Square

Every Christmas, the English National Ballet performs The Nutcracker at the London Coliseum. Over 100 dancers and musicians bring the story to life with exquisite dancing, beautiful sets and Tchaikovsky's glorious score played live.
www.ballet.org.uk

Peter Pan Cup

Serpentine Lake, Hyde Park; 25 December 2022
Nearest Station: South Kensington / Knightsbridge

Members of the Serpentine Swimming Club meet on Christmas Day to compete in the annual 100-yard race on the south bank of the lake. It's happened since 1864 and the Peter Pan author J.M. Barrie donated the cup in 1904. Spectators are welcome.
serpentineswimmingclub.com

MORE DECEMBER 2022 EVENTS

- London International Horse Show: mid-Dec (Annual equestrian event)

- Houses of Parliament Guided Tours
  (During Parliamentary Christmas recess)
- NYE Fireworks: 31 Dec (Stunning
  spectacle focused around the London
  Eye on the River Thames)
- Hyde Park Winter Wonderland: TBD -
  Annual fun fair, German Market located
  in Hyde Park every year.

Do note, probably more than ever before, all of these details are subject to change.

LONDON EXPLORED
PHOTOGRAPHER PETER DAZELEY RETURNS WITH A NEW BEAUTIFUL NEW BOOK
Photography by Peter Dazeley

Peter at work at Crystal Palace

Editor's Note: One of our favorite photographers in Britain is Peter Dazeley. His coffee table books are treasures in my library and he has a new one out this year. He's kindly let us publish a selection of his favorite images from the book to help promote *London Explore: Secrets, Surprising, and Unusual Places to Discover in the Capital.* Thank you Peter!

About the book:

London is packed with little-known treasures: remarkably preserved historical houses, fascinating museums and galleries, unusual commercial and industrial buildings, and sumptuous interiors that are glimpsed only on special occasions.

Take a tour of London's most intriguing locations and see the city as you've never done before with this behind-the-scenes views of the Capital's surprising and hidden places. From deep level bunkers to gin distilleries, ancient water mills to the most lavish casino, London Explored is a unique guidebook that opens the doors to more than sixty locations, revealing a wealth of stories about this endlessly fascinating world city with its own unique character.

This entirely fresh view of the Capital features over 200 stunning images by celebrated photographer Peter Dazeley accompanied by Mark Daly's expert commentary and is a follow-up to the hugely successful Unseen London, London Uncovered and London Theatres, also published by Frances Lincoln and photographed by Dazeley.

PETER DAZELEY BEM FRPS, known as Dazeley, is an acclaimed fine art and advertising photographer whose work has won many awards from organisations across the world, including the Association of Photographers and the Royal Photographic Society in the UK, EPICA in France, Applied Arts Magazine in Canada, and Graphis Inc. in the USA. He is a member of the Association of Photographers and a Fellow of the Royal Photographic Society, and was recognised in the Queen's 2017 New Year's Honours list for his services to photography and charity.

"I'm a born and bred Londoner who thought he knew London incredibly well, yet my fourth book has been another extraordinary journey of discovery for me. So, it is a joy to share the amazing secrets and surprises of my wonderful city in London Explored. I'm seen here photographing one of my favourite locations from the book, the stunning, and rarely seen, Crystal Palace Subway. The Subway supports a four-lane highway and was built to connect Crystal Palace high-level station with the celebrated Crystal Palace building. As befits Victorian thinking, the poor left the station by the front entrance walking up the hill across the road and into the Palace via a public entrance. The rich though, with first class tickets, used the private Crystal Palace Subway under the road and walked directly, via their own private staircase, into the Palace."

MARK DALY is a writer and publisher with a longstanding interest in secret and little-known aspects of London. He has devised a number of London walking tours focussing on unusual and hidden parts of the city and his previous book with Dazeley is the acclaimed Unseen London.

London Explored is the latest in a series published by Frances Lincoln and photographed by Peter Dazeley

Now available from booksellers everywhere.

*1948 Wolseley 18-85 Top Speed 43mph The Metropolitan Police
Historic Vehicle Collection*

Ace Cafe Reunion Weekend September 2019

Lola Love's
SHOOTING GALLERY
Try Your Luck!
THE GARAGE
Rainbow
PHILIPS
CLUB PARADIS
XPRESS
HTER
Gods Own Junk Yard

YOU
Pink Love Cloud
forever
Moishe's
HOME MADE BAKE
ALL THE
FUN
OF THE
FAIR
HOT FOOD
FAM
FUN FUN FUN

Clermont Casino staircase

Animals in War Memorial in Park Lane

A giraffe audience comprising taxidermy heads of Rothschilds reticulated and maasai giraffes Natural History Museum

History Floor The London Library

HISTORY FLOOR
& SCIENCE
HISTORY FLO
DOWN TO
TOPOGRAPHY
DANGER
415 VOLTS

Garden Museum next to Lambeth Palace

Gatricks Temple to Shakespeare on the Bank of the River Thames at Hampton

Liberty of London

Pedway at London Wall

Crystal Palace Subway

Entrance Hall in The Old Lloyds Bank

Interior of 'New' Lloyds of London

Raqib Shaw, The Salon, at the Sausage Factory

Sipsmith Distillery's Copper Pot Stills, named Prudence and Constance

Massive Oak door embellished with the head of Medusa, Crosby
Moran Hall

Hope the blue whale skeleton in the Hintze Hall

Earth Hall
and
Stegosaurus
Free gallery

RNLI crew at Tower Lifeboat Station

*Skeletons Left to Right Goat, Orangutan, Chimpanzee, Human,
Gorilla and Donkey at Grant Museum of Zoology*

The Long Room Purdey and Sons Ltd

The Oranges and Lemons Bells featuring The Sanctus Bell Cast in 1588 the year of the Spanish Armada and called Robertus after Robert Mot who started the Bell Foundry at Whitechapel.

The Deans Staircase better known as the Geometric Staircase in
the south tower St Pauls Cathederal featured in the Harry Potter
Films

Windrush Car Storage, McLaren 720s ready for owner

The Original Great Hall inside Crosby Moran Hall

The Powder Room at Annabels

The Morning Room 18 Stafford Terrace

The Dome St Pauls Cathederal

SOVND OF THE TRVMPET PꝶSE HIM VPON THE LVTE ANDHARP

THE TYPEFACES OF LONDON
A History of Eric Gill and Edward Johnston's Fonts
MANSION HOUSE
PLAISTOW
DAGENHAM EAST
UPMINSTER
IGH ST. KENSINGTON
Platform 2
TOV
STO
BAR
HIGH ST. KE
AND EDGWA
For Notting Hill Gat
take an Edgware Roa

Modernity, when it arrives, manifests itself across all culture. When Britain was leaving behind the Victorian era, everything changed, including the lettering used for communication. Influenced by Roman simplicity and Medieval craftsmanship, there was a movement away from the ornate and melodramatic lettering styles of the Victorians towards cleaner, simpler forms that reflected the times. Edward Johnston, and his student and friend Eric Gill, were influenced by the Arts and Crafts Movement, and Johnston revived, almost single-handedly, the art of penmanship and calligraphy. When the London Underground wanted modern lettering to reflect their modern image, they chose Johnston to create it. Inspired by a column from ancient Rome, he designed a typeface that made the signs and posters of the underground system instantly recognizable. With his new sans-serif lettering owned by the Underground, Eric Gill created a similar typeface, which became just as widely used by British Rail, and it was widely distributed as a modern yet classical typeface for a new century.

William Morris and the Arts and Craft Movement was a 19th-century reaction to the excesses of early industrial production. The Movement promoted traditional craft methods rather than factory production, and it was particularly interested in the Medieval period, when highly-skilled craftsmen worked for themselves, free of factory bosses and production deadlines, to create an object of refinement and beauty. The network of the Movement spread wide and deep, and so there was nothing particularly unusual in the fact that two of Morris' followers, the architect William Harrison Cowlishaw, and William Lethaby, principal of the Central School of Arts and Crafts, both separately met, in 1898, a quiet young man called Edward Johnston.

Johnston was born in Uruguay, but he had been brought up in England by an aunt. His father was a British Cavalry officer, and his mother, Priscilla Buxton, was the daughter of the abolitionist Sir Thomas Fowell Buxton, MP. Home educated, he had followed his own interests and loved mathematics, technology, and practicing the refined handwriting of illuminated manuscripts. When Cowlishaw and Lethaby met him, they encouraged his pursuit of

this almost-lost art and advised him to study works at the British Museum. There he discovered the virtues of the broad-edged pen. Difficult to master, this pen has a flat, split nib, unlike the round nib of a modern ball-point. It allows for variations in the thickness of the line created in a continuous, flowing manner – a ribbon of ink.

Lethaby hired Johnston to teach lettering at the Central School, and in 1906 he published a handbook, Writing & Illuminating, & Lettering. Single-handedly he revived the craft of penmanship and developed techniques still used today by amateur and professional practitioners alike.

Public lettering of the time, such as was seen in the advertisements and posters that covered London, was ornate, exaggerated, and designed for impact rather than grace or beauty. So when the commercial manager of the 'Underground Electric Railways Company of London,' Frank Pick, wanted to create a bold image for the new company, which had amalgamated the various independent lines of the London Underground system, the last thing he wanted was lurid Victorian lettering. In 1913 he approached Johnston, who had tried but failed to break into the business of creating printing fonts, to create a standard font for the systems signs and notices. His main request was that the lettering should be distinct and not be confused with the advertising posters in the stations and passageways.

Seeking inspiration, Johnston turned to the Column of Trajan in Rome, which celebrated the victory of the Emperor Trajan over the Dacia in the first century AD. The Roman lettering on the column

UNDERGROUND
MALLARD
Left Luggage
Toilets
Tickets
London Eye Pier
Underground
Bakerloo, Northern and
Waterloo & City lines
Way out
Station reception
Taxis
First aid point
Station Approach
Way out
Welcome to Waterloo Station
NetworkRail
WAY OUT
STATION CLOSED
AN
LONDON
UNDERGROUND
TRANSPORT

Eric Gill (Left) and Edward Johnston (Right)

was very highly regarded in the Arts & Crafts Movement. It differed from most other lettering by lacking the short lines at the ends of the strokes, called 'serifs,' that characterize many other forms of lettering. This sans-serif letting was already used in the 19th century, but in a very solid, bold form, with thick strokes, today called grotesques, giving a blocky, attention-seeking form. Johnston's, by contrast, was slender but still substantial – he had found the perfect balance. The type also resembled Caslon, which was created in the 18th century by William Caslon, and is considered the first distinctive English typeface.

Johnston's font, variously called Underground or Johnston's Railway Type, but today simply called Johnston, was adopted by the Underground, first for printed material, but later for station signs. Johnston also designed the iconic 'bar and circle' logo still in use today by the Underground system.

Johnston's font survived the various re-organizations of the system until 1979 when it became necessary to re-design it due to changes in printing technology. Eiichi Kono, of the design and typography firm of Banks & Miles, created New Johnston, with a wider range of forms, adding Italics, Medium, and Condensed forms to Johnston's simple originals of Regular in upper and lowercase, and Bold, in uppercase only. This is the font currently used in the system. The original Johnston can be seen in archival materials.

Johnston had a student at the Central School called Eric Gill. Gill had been born in Brighton in 1882. He studied church architecture with William Douglas Caroe, another major figure in the Arts & Crafts Movement, who built numerous early 20th century churches in classic styles. Gill found his studies frustrating, and he turned instead to simultaneously studying stonemasonry and calligraphy – the latter with Johnston. He moved to the countryside and established a sculptor's workshop at the village of Ditchling, Sussex. There he created figures based on ecclesiastic church pieces, such as the Madonna. Johnston and his wife joined him at Ditchling, which

ABCDEFGHIJKLM
NOPQRSTUVWXYZ
abcdefghijklm
nopqrstuvwxyz
1234567890

THE CURRENT ITERATION OF JOHNSTON'S FONT

ABCDEFGHIJKLM
NOPQRSTUVWXYZ
abcdefghijklm
nopqrstuvwxyz
1234567890

became a kind of artist's commune.

Gill's career as a typographer began with a commission for an alphabet for the sign-painters of W.H. Smith's, the stationers, and booksellers. A friend, Stanley Morison, was a historian of type who advised the Monotype Corporation, a typeface company that would later develop the ubiquitous modern types of Times New Roman and Arial. Looking for a san-serif type that would rival new German typefaces, he approached Gill to design something for him. He wanted to combine Gill's style based on letters cut into stone with Johnston's Underground Type. Gill's stated aim was to produce a type that was clean, modern, and classical all at the same time. One easily-noticed difference from Johnston's font is the change from diamond-shaped dots on i and j, replacing them with circular dots. Gill worked on the font between 1927 and 1930.

Morison promoted Gill Sans, as the new type was called, and it was quickly adopted first by the London and North Eastern Railway, and then by British Rail. Penguin Books, always promoters of the modern, adopted it for their book covers, and it became – and remains – one of the most popular type faces in England. Monotype created numerous variations and additions over the years. It is considered particularly attractive in uppercase, and for signage, but less so in lowercase, so it is rarely used for text, for example.

Eric Gill went on to a significant career as a sculptor, moving into Art-Deco, when that became popular in the 1930s. Major works can be seen at the BBC's Broadcast House, and above doorways in London and elsewhere. Gill's legacy is less happy, however, as it was revealed in his personal diaries that he sexually abused his daughters, amongst other depravities. There's a movement to have his statues taken down, and for people to stop using his fonts (and use similar ones instead).

Sites to Visit

Ditchling Museum of Art & Craft, Ditchling, East Sussex, contains work by Gill and Johnston, including material related to their fonts.

The London Transport Museum, in the Covent Garden Piazza, WC2, has numerous pieces in Johnston. The Museum is open until 6 pm every day. The London Transport Depot, Acton, has more, but it is only open for special occasions on a few days a year.

If you want to see both typefaces 'in the wild' you only need to go on a stroll around London - you will find both fonts all around you.

Further Research

- Writing & Illuminating & Lettering, by Edward Johnston
- Edward Johnston: A Signature for London, by Richard Taylor
- Edward Johnston: Master Calligrapher, by Peter Holliday
- Edward Johnston, by Priscilla Johnston
- Eric Gill, by Fiona MacCarthy
- Eric Gill: Man of Flesh and Spirit, by Malcolm Yorke
- An Essay on Typography, by Eric Gill and Christopher Skelton
- Eric Gill, autobiography, by Eric Gill

WHAT LONDON HAS LOST

WHAT DIDN'T SURVIVE THE PANDEMIC

By Laura Porter

FISHERMAN'S FRIEND
SLOW
STAND BY
HALF
AHEAD
FULL
MECHANS
SCOTS
GLASG
DEVOLD
MITTEN
Fantastic top
quality tools
Come in and
have a look!
Double
Noggin the
Nog DVD!
£27.99
FISHERMAN'S FRIEND
cal Almanac
WOLFGANG PETERSEN'S
THE ORIGINAL UNCUT
DIGITALLY REMASTER
12
Spork titanium
ARTHUR BEALE
Marlin's Mission
a talk by
Dave Selby
THE
iMPRACTICAL
BOAT OWNER
THE SAGAS OF
NoGGiN
The NoG
ALPHA · BRAVO

London is always changings, and the pandemic certainly will leave its mark on this great city. The Covid-19 pandemic impacted hospitality, retail, and entertainment when everything had to close for the first lockdown in March 2020. The enforced interrupted trade and financial burden has meant not all businesses have been able to continue and some sadly won't be returning. This list is not exhaustive but it does show us some of the permanently altered London landscape.

Some of these special places may be reborn in another form, some are closed for good, some may try to re-open when the pandemic is 'over.' Hopefully, there aren't a lot of your London favorites on this list!

FOOD AND DRINK

Bar Boulud at the Mandarin Oriental Hotel

After its 10-year lease expired, Bar Boulud at the Mandarin Oriental Hotel closed in October 2020. The restaurant served rustic French bistro-inspired dishes and was best known for its house-made terrines, pâtés and foie gras-stuff burgers by NYC chef Daniel Boulud.
Address: 66 Knightsbridge, London SW1X 7LA

Bubbledogs

This was Sandia Chang's Champagne bar in Fitzrovia that also served gourmet hot dogs. It survived for six years, and the restaurant had been recently refurbished, but Bubbledogs had to close in August 2020. The space is now used by its sister restaurant – Kitchen Table – which is a Michelin-starred dining experience. The Bubbledogs website is still available for online orders of the finest grower Champagnes.
Address: 70 Charlotte Street, London W1T 4QG

Café de Paris

Open since 1924, Café de Paris was a leading London entertainment venue for nearly 100 years. Close to Piccadilly Circus and Leicester Square, this iconic cabaret venue had hosted the likes of Frank Sinatra, Judy Garland, and Noel Coward over

the years. (I once had a very late night there seeing Boy George.) The club closed permanently in December 2020.
Address: 3-4 Coventry Street, London W1D 6BL

Le Caprice

Loved by celebs, this classic St James's restaurant was located near the Royal Academy and Fortnum & Mason. The art deco dining room was a favorite venue of the late Diana, Princess of Wales, who always sat at the same corner table. After 38 years of fine dining, it closed in June 2020. When the closure was announced, there was speculation that the restaurant would reopen at a new site but there has been no more news on that.
Address: 20 Arlington Street, London SW1A 1RJ

Cereal Killer Café

They served 120 different types of breakfast cereal for 5 and a half years, but the twin-brother owners, Alan and Gary Keery, announced they would not reopen in July 2020. The derisive comments when the first of these eateries launched were not enough to hold them back from opening a second branch in Camden. It was retro, it was hipster, but it was fun. The brothers have said 'Cheerio' to the cafes but they have the UK's biggest online range of American cereals available on their website.
Address: Stables Market Mezz, 2 Chalk Farm Road, London NW1 8AH
Address: 192a Brick Lane, London E1 6SA

Crobar

This Soho rock bar has had to close but it is fundraising to try and reopen at a new location after difficulties with rent payments during lockdown. This small but well-loved heavy metal nightspot first opened in 2001 with a loud jukebox and anarchistic atmosphere.
Address: 17 Manette Street, London W1D 4AS

Dinerama

A former truck yard in Shoreditch, this two-level market for street food traders lasted for five years before closing its doors. It did reopen after the first lockdown for a final ten weeks before it had to

stop in October 2020 after failing to reach a rent agreement.
Address: 19 Great Eastern Street, London EC2A 3EJ

Dominique Ansel Bakery

World-famous pastry chef and cronut creator, Dominique Ansel has closed both London locations. The croissant-doughnut hybrid sweet treat was a hit although the bestseller was the DKA – a flaky caramelized croissant. The original branch opened in Belgravia in 2016, and the second branch, Treehouse, opened in Covent Garden in February 2020. It was announced in August 2020 that the two sites, run on license from Dominique Ansel Bakery (DAB) in the US, were deemed unable to be profitable.
Address: 17-21 Elizabeth Street, London SW1W 9RP
Address: 24 Floral Street, London WC2E 9DP

Harry Morgan

This legendary Jewish restaurant and deli in St John's Wood opened back in 1948. They billed themselves as "London's most famous New York-style deli restaurant." It was well-loved for its salt beef, chicken soup, and latkes but decided to close in April 2021 because of a rent dispute with the landlord.
Address: 29-31 St John's Wood High Street, London NW8 7NH

Hung's

If you had ever walked through Chinatown you would have seen the bright red exterior of Hung's and its window display of roast ducks. It relied on night-time trade but with the stay at home orders and initial prejudice about the Chinese origins of the coronavirus, it couldn't survive. It has been closed since October 2020 and people are still talking about the Cantonese roast meats and the Hong Kong dai pai-dong style noodles.
Address: 27 Wardour Street, London W1D 6PR

The Ledbury

15 years in Notting Hill, two Michelin stars and considered to be one of the world's best restaurants, Australian head chef Brett Graham had

to make the heartbreaking decision to close The Ledbury. He knew there was no way to have social distancing inside the restaurant and he announced, "We can't keep customers and staff safe" in June 2020. It is still hoped that a new version of the famous eaterie will open, and there is a new rumor, a more informal brasserie being planned.
Address: 127 Ledbury Road, London W11 2AQ

Milk & Honey

The Milk & Honey cocktail bar was originally founded in New York City in 1999 with another location in London that opened in 2002. The bar was fundamental in establishing the speakeasy trend in London and trained up many of the capital's best cocktail makers. Sadly, this was another venue that had rent disputes that led to its permanent closure.
Address: 61 Poland Street, London W1F 7NU

Milkbar Soho

This speciality coffee shop was connected to the Flat White cafe on Berwick Street. The Milkbar lasted for 12 years on a Soho back street as a small but well-loved cafe. They served Swedish drop coffee and legendary espressos. The Milkbar closed in September 2020.
Address: 3 Bateman Street, London W1D 4AG

Monty's Deli

Monty's has been another casualty of the pandemic after closing its venues in Market Halls and Spitalfields's Kitchen and struggling to keep afloat relying on sandwich meal kits and wholesale sales. Sadly, the New Yoik-style sarnie maestros have called it a day for good. Known for its famous pastrami, salt beef and bagels Londoners and visitors will no longer be able to visit.
225 - 227 Hoxton Street, Hoxton, London N1 5LG

Old Red Cow

This Smithfield Market pub had a decent selection of British craft beers and, as one of the few pubs in the area open on Sundays, they also did a great roast dinner. There was an extra floor upstairs and beer-battered cod & chips was a good choice too.
Address: 71 Long Lane, London EC1A 9EJ

Percy Ingle

This 66-year-old cherished east London bakery chain had 48 sites. While it did reopen after the first lockdown it soon announced a phased closure of all branches. This was a proper working class bakery where you could get a fresh bloomer and a slice of Tottenham cake at prices as good as at a supermarket.
Address: Various London locations include Walthamstow, Leyton, Holloway Road, Hackney, Bethnal Green, and Canning Town.

Piebury Corner

Football fans love a pie and this was the pie shop for Arsenal fans. Both the main branch close to the Emirates Stadium and the Kings Cross spin-off are now closed. It started in 2011 as a stall on match days and the popularity grew to a large cafe a year later. When landlords at both sites asked for full rent, and yet there were no football matches so few customers, they made the decision to close in August 2020.
Address: 209-211 Holloway Road, London N7 8DL

Rivington Greenwich

The Greenwich branch of Richard Caring's Rivington restaurants has also closed (the tycoon owns Caprice Holdings which included Le Caprice.) The Rivington served modern bistro dishes, had an extensive gin menu and had an outdoor dining space.
Address: 178 Greenwich High Road, London SE10 8NN

Rochelle Canteen at The ICA

What started as a cafe in a converted bike shed in Shoreditch in 2006 proved its worth by opening a second branch inside the ICA (Institute of Contemporary Arts) in 2017. Whether you went to the upstairs dining room for modern British fare or the downstairs cafe, there was always a cool creative vibe. The coffee was great and the pies were impressive. Rochelle Canteen at The ICA closed in September 2020 but the east London branch is still open.
Address: The Mall, London SW1Y 5AH

Roux at Parliament Square

This fine-dining restaurant in Westminster run by TV chef Michel Roux Jr. was forced to close for good in December 2020. The head chef, Steve Groves, was the 2009 winner of Masterchef The Professionals and the 2020 National Chef of the Year. Roux still has Le Gavroche, and Roux at The Landau – although it has still not reopened, there are plans for late 2021.
Address: 11 Great George Street, London SW1P 3AD

Shepherdess Café

After 37 years, this Hoxton stalwart was forced to close in July 2020. It was a fantastic 'greasy spoon' known for its full English breakfasts and bright green decor. "Circumstances, Covid-19, increased rents and a lack of sympathy from agents and landlords have all come together and forced the issue."
Address: 221 City Road, London EC1V 1JN

Sticky Fingers

After 32 years, ex-Rolling Stones bassist Bill Wyman permanently closed his Kensington restaurant in June 2021. Sticky Fingers, which took its name from the band's 1971 album, opened in May 1989 and was adorned with a wide selection of Rolling Stones memorabilia.
Address: 1 Phillimore Gardens, London W8 7QB

Sushi Hiroba

This conveyor-belt Japanese sushi restaurant at Holborn was always busy but it couldn't survive the enforced closure.
Address: 50-54 Kingsway, London WC2B 6EP

Terroirs

This central London natural wine bar closed in June 2021. For 13 years, it was a great location, just off Trafalgar Square. The team does still have two London south London sites as Terroirs East Dulwich and Soif (Battersea) are continuing to trade as normal.
Address: 5 William IV Street, London WC2N 4DN

Thomas's Cafe at Burberry

Named after founder Thomas Burberry, Thomas's
Cafe at Burberry was located across two floors
of the 121 Regent Street flagship store in London
with a separate entrance on Vigo Street. This all-day
British classic menus will be missed for its perfect
lobster benedict, the Champagne and oysters, and
the afternoon tea.
Address: 5 Vigo Street, London W1S 3HA

Tibits

Both the Mayfair and Bankside branches of
this vegetarian buffet bar restaurant closed in
September 2020. The small Swiss chain and plant-
based pioneers first arrived in the UK 12 years
ago but will now focus on their operations in
Switzerland and Germany.
Address: 12-14 Heddon Street, London W1B 4DA
Address: 124-128 Southwark Street, London SE1 0SW

Tramshed

In April 2020, Mark Hix's restaurant empire went
into administration. Hix Soho had already closed
in December 2019, so this news meant the loss of
Hixter Bankside, Hix Oyster and Chophouse, and
Tramshed – famous for its whole roast chicken and
Damien Hirst formaldehyde cow. I only got to try
Hix Soho but I loved the contemporary art and
high-quality dining.
*Address: The Tramshed Project, 32 Rivington Street,
London EC2A 3LX*
*Address: Hixter Bankside, 16 Great Guildford Street,
London SE1 0HS*
*Address: Hix Oyster and Chophouse, 36-37 Greenhill
Rents, Cowcross Street, London EC1M 6BN*

Vanilla Black

This was one of London's most innovative and longstanding vegetarian restaurants. For 16 years, Vanilla
Black created incredible plant-based fine dining
but the cost of a central London location during
lockdown was too much and it closed in September
2020. I had lunch there once and have never had
anything anywhere near as exciting in vegetarian
dining. While no longer a restaurant, Vanilla Black
Cook and Learn is now a cooking school offering

online classes.
Address: 17-18 Took's Court, London EC4A 1LB

Wahlburgers

Mark Wahlberg's family US burger and bar chain
opened in London in May 2019 but it only lasted
a year. There had been plans for more branches
across the country but this one Covent Garden
branch was all the UK got.
Address: 8-9 James Street, London WC2E 8BH

Tracks and Records

Another celebrity-backed restaurant, Tracks and
Records was Usain Bolt's Spitalfields-based bar and
restaurant. It launched in London in 2018 with rum
cocktails, live sets from dub and reggae DJs and
Jamaican plates but closed in November 2020.
Address: 94 Middlesex Street, London E1 7EZ

Woodlands

A popular Indian vegetarian restaurant off Leicester
Square, Woodlands had been in London since 1981.

HOTELS

Ace Hotel London Shoreditch

American hotel company Ace Hotel has permanently closed its first hotel outside of the US. The 5-star Ace Hotel London Shoreditch closed in September 2020. This was a hipster hangout with vintage furniture and some rooms had turntables with a selection of vinyl and acoustic guitars.
Address: 100 Shoreditch High Street, London E1 6JQ

Curtain Hotel

The Curtain opened in 2017 under Michael Achenbaum, the New York hotel operator, but closed in October 2020. The hotel has been renamed the Mondrian Shoreditch London, but the Curtain name has been retained on the private members' club. The Curtain Hotel was also home to the first London outpost of Red Rooster, a restaurant from Michelin-star chef Marcus Samuelson, who served as guest chef for Barack Obama's first state dinner as president. The restaurant and bar closed with the hotel.
Address: 45 Curtain Road, London EC2A 3PT

RETAIL

Arthur Beale

It had always seemed incredible that there was a sailing goods shop in Covent Garden but the business is actually 500 years old. The shop started as a rope maker so the location made sense then as in the 16th century large numbers of flax plants were grown in fields in the area which were used to manufacture boat sails and rope. While not many customers went into the shop recently it was still the place for Everest explorers to buy their supplies. The store closed in June 2021 and has found a much more suitable new home at the Portsmouth Historic Dockyard.
Address: 194 Shaftesbury Avenue, London WC2H 8JP

F W Collins

While this hadn't been a hardware shop since 2008, many still remembered it as a place that sold everything. I worked in Covent Garden for a long time so knew the store when Freddie Collins was running it and then when Malcolm Davey took over as a good friend was the shop manager. The Vintage Showroom opened in the building selling vintage clothing from the 1950s to 1990s alongside their up-cycle own-label brand but closed in April 2020.
Address: 14 Earlham Street, London WC2H 9LN

Ian Allan Book and Model Shop

This well-loved transport bookshop near Waterloo station reached the end of the line in October 2020.
Address: 45-46 Lower Marsh, London SE1 7RG

Debenhams

After 242 years of trading, this national chain of department stores closed in May 2021. It started the liquidation process in December 2020 and had tried to keep some stores open but the high street favorite held closing down sales and is now gone. Online fashion retailer Boohoo bought the Debenhams brand in January 2021.
Address: 334-348 Oxford Street, London W1C 1JG

Habitat

The flagship Habitat store on Tottenham Court Road closed after 50 years at the central London location. The owners, Sainsbury's, have kept some stores to be set up as showrooms but expect most of the sales to be online. This was a wonderful place for home decor inspiration.
Address: 196-199 Tottenham Court Road, London W1T 7PJ

Paperchase

The flagship Paperchase store on Tottenham Court Road is also gone as over half of the Paperchase stores in London were closed to try to safeguard jobs at the surviving branches.
While several of its station stores had to close, Paperchase's shop in London's Victoria Station has remained open.
Address: 213-215 Tottenham Court Road, London W1T 7PS

Top Shop

It was announced in February 2021 that the three-story fashion emporium on Oxford Circus would not be reopening. Nor would any of the other Top Shop branches. Top Shop has been bought by online retailer ASOS who also acquired Top Man and Miss Selfridge. Sports retailers and even IKEA have expressed strong interest in the landmark location.
Address: 214 Oxford Street, Oxford Circus, London W1W 8LG

CULTURE

Florence Nightingale Museum

The Florence Nightingale Museum was the last museum I visited before the pandemic took hold as it has put together a special exhibition for Florence Nightingale's bicentenary. It's at St Thomas' Hospital which is where Boris Johnson was treated when he caught Covid-19 and it's named after a pioneer of handwashing for hygiene. For now, the museum is opening one weekend each month and is having a major review of its operations.
Address: St Thomas' Hospital, 2 Lambeth Palace Road, London SE1 7EW

Bond in Motion @ London Film Museum

This popular James Bond themed exhibition of cars and movie props has closed permanatnly (the space is now occupied by a Harry Potter exhibition).
London Film Museum, 45 Wellington Street, Covent Garden, London WC2E 7BN

A VERY LONDON TV SHOW
Only Fools and Horses

'Only fools and horses work for a living' was the obscure expression the working-class writer John Sullivan chose for the title. His sitcom follows the ups and downs of an illegal street trader, Del Boy, his younger brother, and Grandad, as they attempt to escape from both poverty and class, a hopeless task on both counts, although, in the end, wealth proves easier to achieve than entry in the higher classes of English society. Del's many 'get rich quick' schemes provide endless comic opportunities, and Sullivan's finely observed characters grow and evolve as the seasons flow by, with the ups and downs of real life, seen through a satirical and comic lens.

Although locked into a complex class structure, the British are still able to laugh equally at the foibles of all its social groups. Shows like 'Steptoe & Son' and 'Till Death us do Part' in the 1960s aimed at the working class, while the later 'Spitting Image' skewered Royalty with a sharp spear. The foibles of the working class, though, have always been a rich source for comedy writers, and the appeal of the social faux pas for comic effect is always tempting. The bustling street markets of London, and the eccentricities of the street trader, were the inspiration for Only Fools and Horses, a TV comedy series that ran throughout the 1980s and that was voted 'Britain's Best Sitcom' in 2004.

Only Fools and Horses follows the daily life of market trader Derek 'Del Boy' Trotter, his younger brother Rodney, and their Grandad, as they struggle to find the wealth to escape their life in Peckham, a working-class neighborhood of south-east London. They live in a council flat in Nelson Mandala House, a grim high-rise apartment building, and ever since their mother died when the boys were young, and their father left shortly afterwards, Derek has been the family head and provider, surviving by buying and selling odd items that may have 'fallen of the back of a truck' or have come his way under other doubtful circumstances. His goal is to become a millionaire with some dubious scheme or other, and these plans – always unsuccessful – form the basis of the plots, which usually occupy a single episode. Only later in the series did longer story arcs begin, and a broader picture of their lives and surrounding society emerged. By the end of the series a viewer has gained a rich picture of the back-stories of

<table>
<tr><td colspan="2">

Key Facts

</td></tr>
<tr><td>•</td><td>Six seasons shown, between 1981 and 1999, plus specials</td></tr>
<tr><td>•</td><td>Starred David Jason as Derek' Del Boy' Trotter, Nicholas Lyndhurst as Rodney Trotter, and Lennard Pierce as Grandad</td></tr>
<tr><td>•</td><td>Voted Britain's Best Sitcom in 2004</td></tr>
<tr><td>•</td><td>Written by John Sullivan, who grew up in working-class Balham</td></tr>
<tr><td>•</td><td>Developed a strong cult following and contributed to English slang</td></tr>
</table>

the characters, and this 'epic novel' character of the show is a secondary strength to its immediate comedy.

The accuracy of the characters is guaranteed, since the writer, John Sullivan, grew up in Balham, another south London working-class area. His father was a plumber, and he remembers always being fascinated by the bottom end of the street market scene and particularly the men variously called: 'spivs'; 'fly traders' (because they traded 'on the fly' to dodge the authorities); or, later, 'readies' (ready for anything). Often selling out of suitcases they opened on the street, these characters were Sullivan's inspiration for Derek Trotter. Sullivan had left school unqualified, and eked out a living as a young man in a variety of unskilled jobs, from messenger boy to window cleaner and carpet layer. He persisted in submitting scripts to the BBC, finding his first success with Citizen Smith, and then being commissioned to create Only Fools and Horses.

The show was first aired on the 8th of September 1981, and the first season ran for six episodes, each of 30 minutes. Further seasons, usually also of 6 episodes, ran in 1982, 1983, 1985, 1986, 1989, and 1990. In addition, almost every year there was a Christmas Special episode, and in 1996 three one-hour episodes ran as a Christmas Trilogy. Each Christmas Day of 2001, 2002, and 2003, additional 75 minutes specials were shown. As well, there were a variety of sketches, promotional pieces and other shorts created between 1992 and 2015.

The story arc follows 'Del Boy' (played by David Jason) in his cheap gold jewelry and camel coat as he strives to become rich, eventually achieving that, and then losing most of it again. His business, Trotters Independent Traders (T.I.T.), operates out of a suitcase, or from the back of his yellow three-wheel van. By the end of the series he has begun to emulate the richer 'yuppies' who are gentrifying his neighborhood. After a succession of failed relationships, he eventually meets his 'significant other' in a late episode. Rodney typifies the working-class man who struggles to present himself as 'classier' – an effort always doomed to failure in a society with an acute ear for the subtle cues of class. He affects knowledge he lacks, in particular attempting to use basic French, but always wrongly. When on holiday in Spain (a stereotype working-class destination), he takes a 'fiesta' after lunch. Much of the humor in the series lies in the knowing way an English person will see through these ultimately pathetic attempts to be what he is not.

His brother Rodney (played by Nicholas Lyndhurst) struggles to free himself from Derek's control, and looks scornfully on the shady ways Derek tries to become rich. Rodney did well in school, but was expelled from Art College for smoking cannabis, and now struggles to become independent. He finds himself a middle-class girlfriend, Cassandra (played by Gwyneth Strong), who lives on the fashionable King's Road. Even though he lies about his background she takes to him, and their relationship and marriage continues through the later seasons.

The foil to the younger generations is Grandad (played by Lennard Pierce), who is a stereotypical infirm 'OAP' – old age pensioner – who watches TV all day and is generally abused and derided by his grand-children. When Pierce died in 1984 Grandad was buried, and his place taken by Uncle Albert (played by Buster Merryfield), who can always be relied upon for a story that begins, "During the war. . ." When Merryfield died in 1999, his character also died, and his ashes were scattered in the English Channel.

By the sixth series the writer wanted Del Boy to give up chasing younger girls and settled down, so he created Racquel (played by Tessa Peake-Jones), a woman Del meets through a dating agency. Kind-hearted like Del, but also a failure, she has tried to be an actress, but more often works as a stripagram. By the end of the series they are still not married, although Del seems interested in settling down.

Minor characters in the series include Trigger (Roger Lloyd-Pack and Lewis Osborne), who is a street-sweeper and not too bright. He is a regular at the local pub, the Nags Head, and his father, "Died a few years before he was born." Boycie (John Challis) is a successful used-car salesman, and the richest man at the Nag's Head, while Denzil (Paul Barber) is a long-distance lorry driver and regular victim of Del's get-rich schemes. The crooked policeman, DCI Slater (Jim Broadbent) only appears in three episodes, but is a regular presence in the background of the series.

Cultural Impact

Initial viewing figures for the show were well below 10 million, but by the end of the third series that barrier had been broken, and it eventually peaked at 24.3 million for the third episode of the 1996 Christmas trilogy – over 40% of the national population at the time. After it was voted Britain's Best Sitcom in 2004, several 'Story of. . .' documentaries were produced. Two spin-off series, The Green, Green Grass and Rock & Chips were produced in the early 21st century, and a stage-play version was launched in February 2019 at the Theatre Royal Haymarket, London. Two board games based on the show were also created. The show has also won numerous popularity awards, and it ranks high in polls of the greatest TV shows ever.

The show has been viewed internationally, with particular interest in the countries of the former Yugoslavia, where the show is called Mućke, meaning 'shady deals.' It was remade in The Netherlands as Wat schuift't? (What's it worth?), and in Portugal and Slovenia. Several attempts to launch a US remake have been made, only to be rejected in their final stages.

The 'Only Fools and Horses Appreciation Society' was launched in 1993, with around 7,000 members. It releases a quarterly newsletter, and it has annual conventions of fans and cast members. It also stages Shows featuring props form the show. Such as the yellow van.

Several of the tag lines from the series have entered everyday speech in England, such as 'Plonker' (a fool or idiot), 'Cushty' (good, delightful), and 'Lovely jubbly.' The show has reinforced cultural stereotypes of working-class people and habits, as well as disarming them by turning those elements into comedy memes.

Places to Visit

- London still has many street markets, but most have been gentrified in various ways, and may give only a limited picture of the flavor of traditional markets.
- Deptford Market is near 'Del territory,' and this basic market of food and cheap goods runs from 7 am to 4 pm, Wednesday, Friday, and Saturday, on Deptford High Street.
- Brick Lane Market is held on Sundays from 9 am to 5 pm, and it has a range of goods. This traditional east-end market has gone upscale to a degree, and today incorporates the nearby Truman Market.
- Petticoat Lane Market operates every weekday, and Sunday mornings. It is primarily a clothing market, with much of the old atmosphere. It is situated in Spitalfields, near Aldgate Tube Station. A Sunday visit could include the nearby Columbia Road Flower Market.

- Although set in Peckham, most of the show, and all the later series, were filmed in Bristol. Several small companies offer tours of outdoor locations.
- Tower blocks in the UK have gone from being desirable council housing when first built in the 1950s, to scenes of social decay, and back to desirable housing again, today in private hands. Towers such as Trellick Tower (Kensal Town), Keeling House (Bethnal Green), Sivill House (Shoreditch) and The Barbican Estate (City of London) are admired and desirably homes for young professionals in particular. Many are iconic, listed buildings, and examples of British brutalist architecture.

Where to Watch

- Complete collections of all the series of 'Only Fools and Horses' are available on DVD.
- Netflix is currently not steaming the series, but it is available on Amazon Prime, with a Britbox purchase.
- All episodes of the show are available for download purchase on iTunes.

Further Research

- "The Only Fools and Horses Story, by Steve Clark, 1996
- "The Complete A-Z of Only Fools and Horses, by Richard Weber, 2003
- The Bible of Peckham. a three-volume edition of all the scripts, 2017
- He Who Dares..., by Jim Sullivan, a fictional autobiography of Derek Trotter, 2015
- You Know It Makes Sense, Lessons from The Derek Trotter School of Business (And Life), by Jim Sullivan, 2018
- The People: The Rise and Fall of the Working Class, 1910-2010, by Selina Todd
- The Myth of Meritocracy: Why Working-Class Kids Still Get Working-Class Jobs, by James Bloodworth

A PARTY FIT FOR A QUEEN
GUIDE TO THE PLATINUM JUBILEE CELEBRATIONS
BY LAURA PORTER

In 2022, Her Majesty The Queen will become the first British Monarch to celebrate a Platinum Jubilee. Queen Elizabeth II acceded to the throne on 6 February 1952 when just 25 years old and will have given an incredible seventy years of service.

Throughout 2022 there will be Platinum Jubilee celebrations all over the United Kingdom to celebrate The Queen's historic reign. Such events help reinforce the Sovereign's role as a focus for national identity, and unity as people across the Commonwealth come together to mark an important occasion for their Head of State.

Members of the Royal Family will travel around the country to undertake a variety of engagements to mark this historic occasion culminating with the focal point of the Platinum Jubilee Weekend in June 2022.

Even though February will be the official anniversary marking the Queen's 70-year reign, as with the Queen's Golden and Diamond Jubilees, the first week in June has been chosen for the celebratory weekend, with the summer offering a better chance of good weather.

The Queen will be 96 at the time of the Platinum Jubilee events. Her real birthday is on 21 April, but we celebrate her official birthday in June. 2022 is set to be a blockbuster year, bursting with national pride and showcasing the best of Britain to the world.

Extra Bank Holiday

We usually have a public holiday on the last Monday of June for Whitsun (Pentecost) but that's moved for 2022 and we have gained an extra day off. Instead of the Monday, we've got a Spring Bank Holiday on Thursday 2 June and the extra day is Friday 3 June for the Platinum Jubilee Bank Holiday.

This four-day Jubilee weekend will provide an opportunity for people to come together to celebrate the historic milestone. There are lots of public events planned as well as national moments of reflection on the Queen's 70 years of service.

What Is Planned?

The official commemorations are being arranged jointly with The Royal Household and the Department for Digital, Culture, Media and Sport. The four-day celebrations will reflect on Her Majesty's reign and her impact on the UK and the world since 1952. This historic event will feature an extensive programme that combines the best of British ceremonial splendor and pageantry with cutting edge artistic and technological displays. We are being promised a spectacular weekend of celebrations for a truly historic moment that deserves a celebration to remember.

It is not clear which events the Queen will attend or take part in as she was ordered to rest by doctors in October 2021 following an overnight hospital stay for unspecified preliminary investigations. The bulk of the Jubilee duties are thought likely to be given to the rest of the royal family, including the Prince of Wales and Duchess of Cornwall.

The Queen usually spends the anniversary of her accession privately at Sandringham. Sandringham and Balmoral will both be open for residents and visitors to enjoy the celebrations across the long weekend.

January: Platinum Pudding Competition

The official Jubilee celebrations began on 10 January 2022 when Fortnum & Mason launched the Platinum Pudding Competition to find a dish to dedicate to the Queen's 70 years on the throne. Recipes will be judged by an expert panel, including Dame Mary Berry.

May: A Gallop Through History

From 12th to 15th May 2022, more than 500 horses and 1,000 performers will take part in a 90-minute show taking the Windsor Castle audience through history right from Elizabeth I to the present day.

THURSDAY 2ND JUNE 2022

The Queen's Birthday Parade (Trooping the Colour): This event usually takes place on the second Saturday of June to mark the Queen's official birthday but for 2022 it will be on Thursday 2 June to start the long weekend of celebrations. The color will be trooped on Horse Guards Parade by the 1st Battalion, Irish Guards, and over 1,200 officers and soldiers from the Household Division who will put on a display.

The Parade begins at Buckingham Palace and travels down The Mall to Horse Guard's Parade to arrive at 11 am. Trooping of the Colour is the official inspection of the guards and then the Royal Family travel back to the Palace to watch the traditional RAF fly-past from the Buckingham Palace balcony at 1 pm.

Platinum Jubilee Beacons: The United Kingdom's long tradition of celebrating Royal Jubilees, weddings and coronations with the lighting of beacons will be continued to mark the Platinum Jubilee.

More than 1,500 beacons will be lit throughout the United Kingdom, Channel Islands, Isle of Man and UK Overseas Territories at the same time as the principal beacon at Buckingham Palace. For the first time, beacons will also be lit in each of the capital cities of the Commonwealth countries as well.

FRIDAY 3RD JUNE 2022

Service of Thanksgiving: A Service of Thanksgiving for The Queen's reign will be held at St Paul's Cathedral.

SATURDAY 4TH JUNE 2022

The Derby at Epsom Downs: Her Majesty The Queen, accompanied by members of the Royal Family, will attend the Cazoo Derby at Epsom Downs in Surrey. It is Britain's richest flat horse race. Her Majesty has long enjoyed the thrill of horse racing and she owns many thoroughbred horses for use in racing.

Platinum Party at the Palace: In the evening, the

BBC will stage and broadcast a special live concert from Buckingham Palace. Some of the world's greatest entertainers are billed to perform at the concert at Buckingham Palace to celebrate the most significant moments from the Queen's reign. Members of the public will be invited to apply to attend this special event via a ballot for UK residents.

SUNDAY 5TH JUNE 2022

The Big Jubilee Lunch: The annual Big Lunch began in 2009 to encourage communities to celebrate their connections and get to know each other better. In 2022 The Big Lunch is inviting friends and neighbors to share food and fun as part of the Platinum Jubilee celebrations so we can expect to see plenty of street parties.

The Platinum Jubilee Pageant: This event will round off four days of public celebrations to mark the Queen's record-breaking 70 years on the throne. The Platinum Pageant tells the story of The Queen's long reign and our transforming society. The carnival-style pageant featuring more than

5,000 people from across the United Kingdom and the Commonwealth, includes a trapeze artist suspended beneath a huge helium balloon.

The procession, which is in three acts, will travel through the streets of Westminster and along the Mall past Buckingham Palace. Schoolchildren across the country have been invited to create a picture of their hopes for the planet over the next 70 years, and some of their designs will be put onto the 200 silk flags that create a River of Hope.

The first act is a military spectacle with marching bands and the second act will tell the story of the Queen's reign and how society has transformed throughout the decades. An original story by writer Sir Michael Morpurgo called 'There Once is a Queen' will be brought to life and the parade will feature music, dance, and impressive puppets such as colossal 'Queen's Beasts' the height of three-story houses and dragons with the dimension of London buses. The third act, the Finale of the grand celebrations of the Pageant, will be revealed in 2022.

The organizers tell us, it is no coincidence that the Platinum Jubilee Pageant falls on World Environment Day on 5 June 2022. Sustainability will be considered throughout the planning of the Pageant.

July: The Royal Collection Trust

From July, three displays marking the Queen's accession to the throne, the Coronation and Jubilees will be put on at official royal residences: Buckingham Palace, Windsor Castle, and the Palace of Holyroodhouse.

The Queen's Green Canopy

Launched in May 2021, people across the United Kingdom have been encouraged to 'Plant a Tree for the Jubilee.' This unique tree-planting initiative, created to mark Her Majesty's Platinum Jubilee, is to help the environment and make local areas greener by planting trees from October 2021, when the tree planting season begins, through to the end of the Jubilee year in 2022. The idea is to create a legacy in honour of The Queen which will benefit future generations.

As well as inviting the planting of new trees, The Queen's Green Canopy will dedicate a network of 70 Ancient Woodlands across the United Kingdom and identify 70 Ancient Trees to celebrate Her Majesty's 70 years of service.

Jubilee Emblem

The Royal Household in partnership with the Victoria and Albert Museum (V&A) invited young people aged 13 – 25 to design an emblem for The Queen's Platinum Jubilee in 2022.

The chosen emblem design is based on an original illustration drawn by Edward Roberts, a 19-year-old student at the University of Leeds. The emblem features a purple and platinum design. The continuous platinum line reveals a stylized St Edward's Crown, incorporating the number 70, on

a round purple background associated with royalty and signifying a royal seal. The elegant font Perpetua, meaning forever, is an acknowledgment to the first British Monarch ever to mark 70 years on the throne.

Jubilee Medal

In keeping with tradition, a Platinum Jubilee medal will be awarded to people who work in public service including representatives of the Armed Forces, the emergency services and the prison services. This tradition stretches back to the reign of Queen Victoria when an official medal was designed to mark her 50th anniversary on the throne.

Royal Jubilees

Few British Monarchs have achieved reigns of 50 years. Henry III, Edward III and James VI and I reached the 50-year milestones but there are no records of how it was celebrated. The first British Monarch to mark 50 years on the throne in a significant way was George III, followed by Queen Victoria.

Queen Elizabeth II has had significant Jubilee celebrations in 1977 (for her Silver Jubilee), 2002 (for her Golden Jubilee) and 2012 (for her Diamond Jubilee).

During the summer months in 1977, the Queen embarked on a large-scale tour, having decided that she wished to mark her Jubilee by meeting as many of her people as possible. No other Sovereign had visited so much of Britain in the course of just three months. I remember the street parties, seeing the Queen on the news everywhere and a lot of flag-waving.

A packed program of events took place in 2002 to celebrate fifty years of The Queen's reign. Six key Jubilee themes shaped events: Celebration, Community, Service, Past and future, Giving thanks and Commonwealth. The Queen and The Duke of Edinburgh undertook extensive tours of the Commonwealth and the UK.

2012 was a bumper year for national pride as we had the Diamond Jubilee plus the London 2012 Olympic and Paralympic Games. The Diamond Jubilee was marked with a spectacular central weekend and a series of regional tours. The Queen and The Duke of Edinburgh traveled as widely as possible across England, Scotland, Wales and Northern Ireland, visiting every region during 2012 whilst other members of the Royal Family visited all of the Commonwealth realms (countries where The Queen is Head of State) between them.

6 February 2017 marked 65 years since The Queen acceded to the throne, becoming the first British Monarch to mark their Sapphire Jubilee, although I don't remember us having any national celebrations.

Souvenirs

The earliest known English commemorative items date from the Restoration of Charles II as king in 1660, followed by his Coronation in 1661 and wedding in 1662. You can be sure there will be plenty of souvenirs to mark the Platinum Jubilee, including coins and stamps.

The Royal Mint has released two collectible coins designed by John Bergdahl. The 50p coin shows the Queen on horseback and the £5 crown features a regal design centralized by the quartered shield of the Royal Arms. Both coins feature the portrait of the Queen designed by Jody Clark.

Commemorative coins are not intended for general use and are almost always collected in uncirculated mint condition. Special issue coins were first used to mark a Royal Jubilee with the Golden Jubilee of Queen Victoria in 1887. The first stamps associated with a royal event were those issued in 1887 although they were not intended as commemorative issues.

Ceramics have also proved popular for Jubilee souvenirs. Commemorative items survive in significant numbers from the reign of George III onwards, taking advantage of industrialized production methods such as transfer prints to produce affordable items including mugs, bowls, plaques, jugs and urns.

I think we can safely expect to find commemorative mugs and tea towels selling well in 2022. I'm still using my Golden Jubilee tea towel so I could do with a replacement.

Extra Information

Bhumibol Adulyadej was the most recent Monarch to celebrate a Platinum Jubilee in 2016. Sadly, he died shortly after official celebrations in Thailand took place.

Superbloom is a Commonwealth-themed garden in the historic moat of the Tower of London. In spring 2022, over 20 million seeds will be sown in the moat establishing the first stage of a permanent transformation of the moat into a new natural landscape in the heart of the City of London. Open from June to September 2022, visitors can wander along a weaving path into the center of the flowers accompanied by a specially-commissioned sound installation and sculptural elements.

South Gloucestershire Council has suggested that the Severn Bridge be renamed in honor of The Queen's Jubilee in 2022.

And don't forget about The Queen's Diamond Jubilee Galleries at Westminster Abbey in the stunning 13th-century triforium. Opened in 2018, the galleries showcase artifacts spanning the abbey's remarkable 1000-year history.

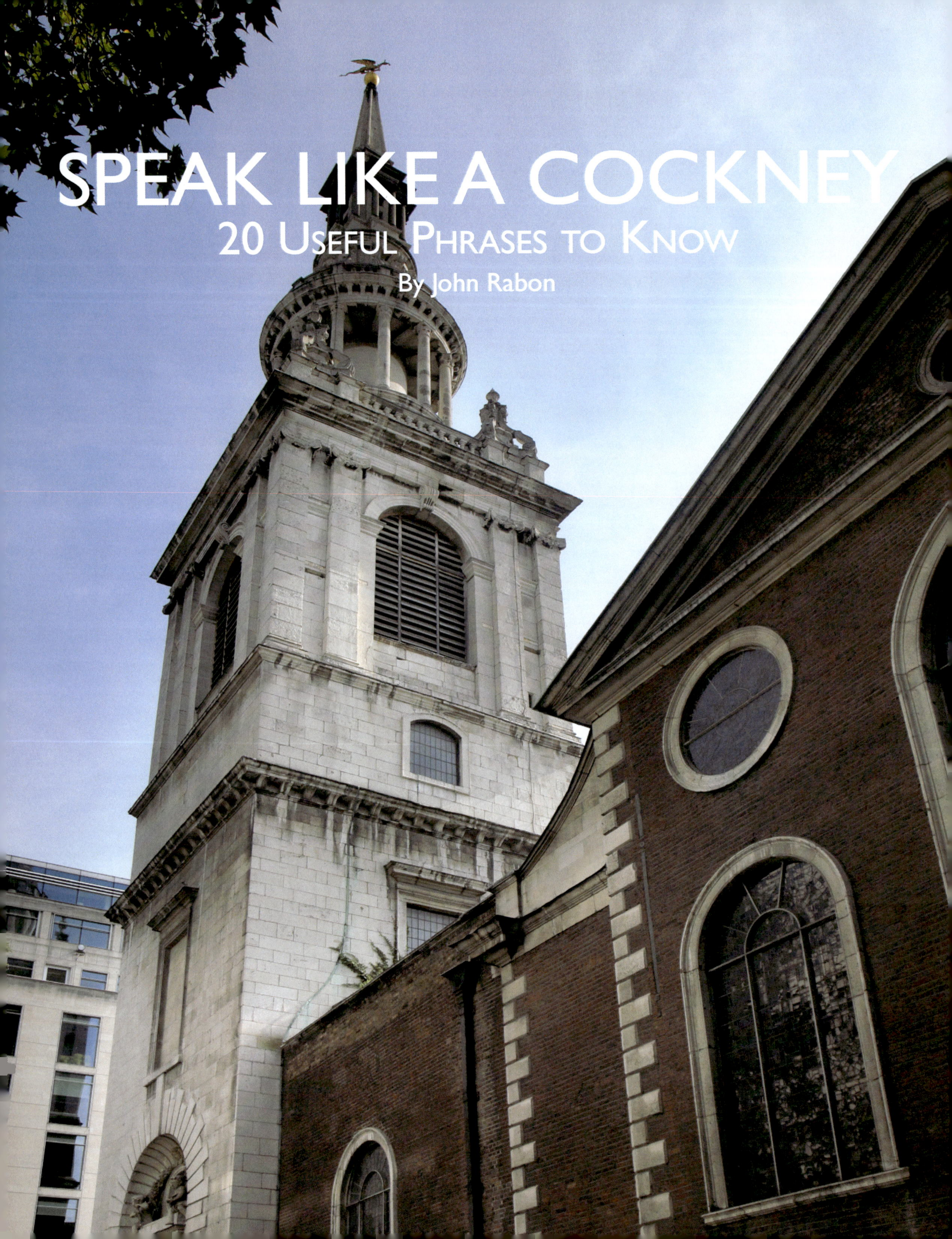

SPEAK LIKE A COCKNEY
20 Useful Phrases to Know
By John Rabon

Cockney rhyming slang has been around since the 19th Century as a special language focused in the East End of London. Debates about the origins focus on whether it was a simple shorthand used by market vendors or a code to cover for criminal activity. Regardless of the reason why rhyming slang started, it became an indelible part of Cockney culture and identity. If you find yourself a bit lost trying to understand the words and phrases that come with this unique London language, we've highlighted twenty Cockney rhyming slang phrases and their meanings below.

Apples and Pears

"Apples and Pears" is a rhyme for "steps and stairs." In the days of the costermongers (market stall owners) in the early 19th Century, the stall owners often had their fruits and vegetables on gradations for display. This display style was also called "steps and stairs," and the rhyme became synonymous with the goods themselves.

Pig's Ear

Certainly not a literal pig's ear; this is a rhyming slang way of saying "beer." This was originally a much longer rhyming phrase, "tiddly wink of pig's ear," which meant "drink of beer." There's no real reason for this beyond being a good rhyme (as is the case with most Cockney slang), and there are several other rhyming words and phrases for beer.

Box of Toys

A "box of toys" is another way of saying noise. The origin is owed to a box of toys making a loud noise when kids are going through them looking for the toy they want most.

Trouble and Strife

This is a rhyming phrase that might get a lot of husbands in trouble if their partners heard it because it is a rhyme for wife. It's not hard to figure out how this one got started since some husbands tend to consider their spouses as the source of a lot of their grief (though it's usually self-inflicted).

Pie and Mash

"Pie and Mash" as a phrase simply refers to money as it rhymes with "cash." It also has a much cruder meaning in that it also rhymes with "slash," which is a much vulgar way of saying "urinate," so be careful to note how it's being used.

Dicky/Dickie

Dicky is one of those Cockney terms that's a shortened form of a longer phrase. Dicky is short for "dicky bird," which around the 1700s meant any small bird common in the UK like a sparrow or chickadee. By the time Cockney rhyming slang came around a century later, they used the "bird" as a rhyme for "word." Telling someone, "You've got my dicky" is the same as making a promise.

Cobblers Awls

This phrase is a bit more blue-collar and is a rhyme for "balls." A similar English slang term is "bollocks," which tends to be used for calling out a lie (ala, "That's a load of bollocks"). Cobblers awls is used in the same way and often shortened to simply "cobblers."

Rosie Lee

If someone offers you a cuppa Rosie Lee, it would be good manners to take it. This is because Rosie Lee is a rhyming slang phrase for tea. The phrase first appeared in print in 1925 and is sometimes shortened to simply "Rosie."

Barcardi Breezer

This is a phrase that can have a couple of meanings based on its rhyme. One is a substitute for "geezer" (a very old person), and the other can describe their freezer. It just goes to show that sometimes you really have to pay attention to the context in which the Cockney is using the slang.

Crowded Space

This is a rhyme referring to a suitcase, which can sometimes be pretty crowded depending on how many things you pack into it for a trip.

North and South

If you're ever told to shut your north and south, that's because it rhymes with mouth. This phrase can have more positive uses, but a fair amount of the time, it's used on people who are talking too much, bragging, or getting way ahead of themselves.

Tom Cruise

Cockneys aren't talking about the movie star when they refer to a Tom Cruise but are actually referring to a bruise. Given the real Tom Cruise's penchant for doing his own stunts and seriously injuring himself in the process (such as when he broke his leg filming Mission Impossible: Fallout), his name not only rhymes well with bruise but is quite appropriate.

Barney Rubble

Fans of the Oceans movie trilogy might recognize this phrase as used by Mockney Don Cheadle's character Basher Tarr. Far from referring to Fred Flintstone's co-worker and best buddy, Barney Rubble is a rhyme for "trouble." Normally, Cockneys will leave off the surname and just say something like, "Well, that looks like Barney."

King Dick

King Dick is not as bad of an insult as Americans might think, but it's still certainly an insult. King Dick is a rhyme for another British insult: "thick." Thick normally means someone who isn't very smart or is particularly dense. If you're being called a King Dick, it means someone thinks you're dumb.

Mickey Mouse

Oh, boy! Naturally, no Cockney is actually referring to Disney's most famous character when they say "Mickey Mouse" or shorten it to "Mickey." In Cockney rhyming slang, this means "house," though "Taking the Mickey" in English slang is similar to "taking the piss," which means to mock someone or something.

Adam and Eve

Adam and Eve can have two different meanings in Cockney rhyming slang, neither of which are Biblical. The first and most common is "believe," as in "I can't Adam and Eve it." The other meaning is "leave," which can be either just going or having to beat a hasty departure.

The first originated as far back as the late 19th Century, while the second came about around the 1930s.

April Showers

If you remember the old phrase "April showers bring May flowers," you're not far off from the meaning of this Cockney phrase. April showers is a shorthand way of saying flowers, and sometimes you can shorten it to say, "I got my girl some Aprils for Valentine's Day."

Dog and Bone

Our final Cockney rhyming slang phrase is a simple rhyme that means "telephone."

Half-inch

This phrase came about in the 1920s and is a rhyme for "pinch." Of course, this doesn't mean a pinch like most of us would think, but pinch is itself a slang term for meaning "steal." As an example, you might hear someone say, "Oy, my wallet's been half-inched!"

Didgeridoo

Nothing to do with the Australian musical instrument, "didgeridoo," in this case, is simple rhyming slang for "clue," as in "I haven't got a didgeridoo where your keys got off to." This doesn't really have a discernable origin and appears to be another rhyme that came about because it sounded similar.

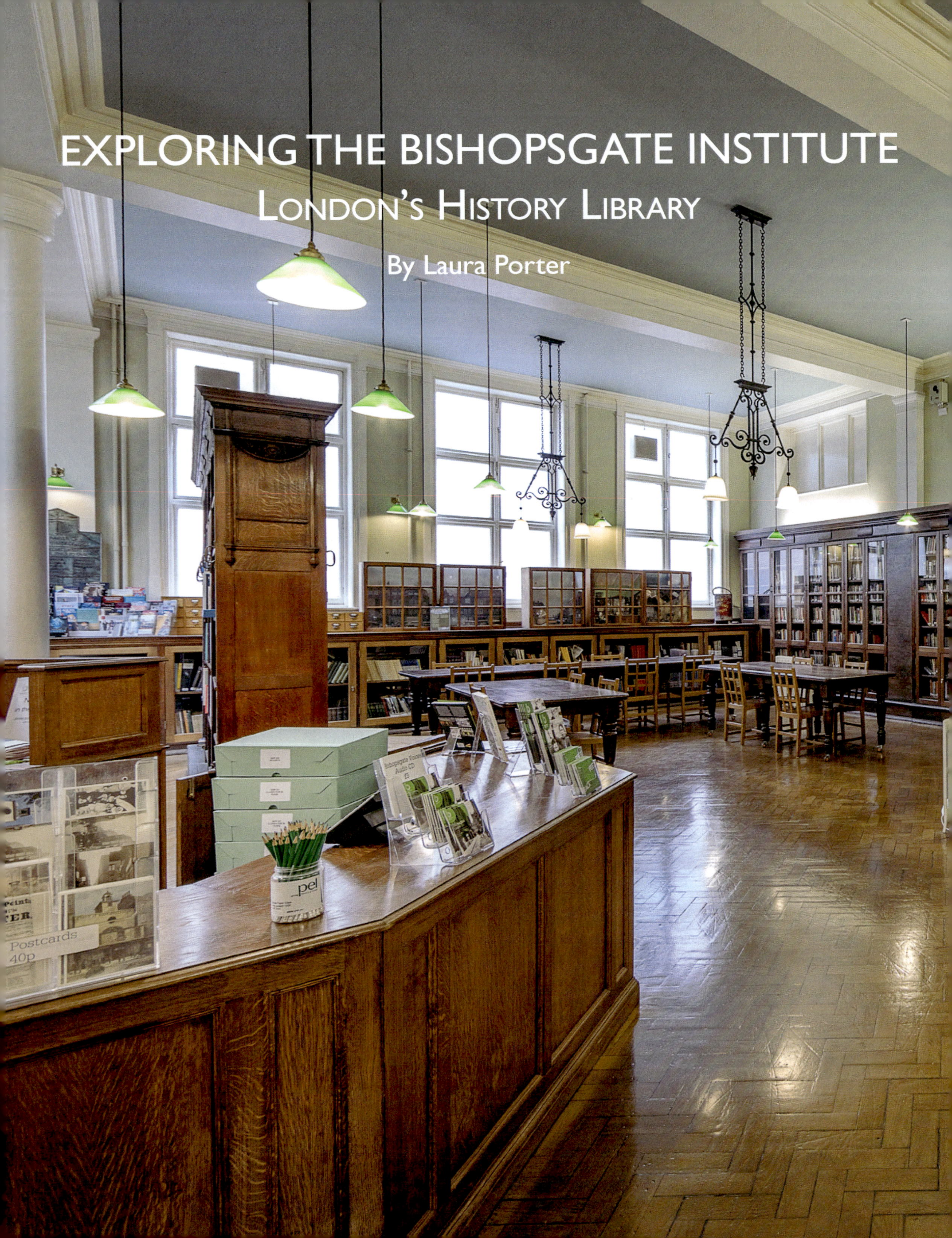

EXPLORING THE BISHOPSGATE INSTITUTE
LONDON'S HISTORY LIBRARY
By Laura Porter

Bishopsgate Institute was certainly somewhere I was aware of. I'd walked past loads of times and had even gone inside once but did I know the place well? No, I did not.

So when a friend asked if I'd seen the suffragette tea set held in the archives there, I knew I had to find out more. What sort of place keeps a suffragette tea set? Or a hand-painted mask of a black MP? Or extensive press clippings about a previous Head of Scotland Yard? It was all too intriguing, so I arranged to meet Stefan Dickers, Special Collections and Archives Manager at Bishopsgate Institute.

Flat-cap wearing Archivist Stefan has worked here since 2005 and has seen the archive grow dramatically. There are now four large underground archive rooms with the full collection held on-site. And as we toured the library and archives, I discovered he could rattle off dates and locations from his encyclopedic knowledge.

What is Bishopsgate Institute?

Bishopsgate Institute is a cultural location with adult talks, workshops, and events, as well as the extensive library and archives. You could take a course in Lindy Hop dancing or learn a new language, go on a weekend walking tour of the East End, study poetry about London or try a photography workshop on the nearby streets. There are regular Archive Tours, and anyone can use the library, which has an incredible London books collection.

It has been open since 1895 as "a home for ideas and debate, learning and inquiry; a place where culture, heritage, and learning meet, and where independent thought is cherished." It does sound good, doesn't it?

The site of the Bishopsgate Institute straddles the eastern fringe of the City of London. It's opposite Liverpool Street Station and close to Spitalfields Market.

Bishopsgate Institute was "erected for the benefit of the public" after the local churches were encouraged to do something for the community with all the donations they received. William Rogers, the Rector of St Botolph's from 1863 to 1896, was a great social reformer and immediately agreed to the idea of a library and place of learning for all. He had already founded schools for the poor of the neighborhood, established soup kitchens in the winter for the army of casual laborers attracted by the railway work, and erected public drinking fountains for clean water.

The new scheme wasn't appreciated by everyone. Blackwood's Magazine suggested the library would be for "louts" to have "a nice warm room in which to read the worst novels and the sporting news in the papers and neglect their natural work!"

The plan was to have a lending library with 50,000 volumes (of which some 20,000 were already on the shelves at the opening) and a reference library for 10,000 volumes.

It was certainly wanted by the local population as 4,500 application forms were issued to potential borrowers on the first day. By Easter 1895, it was reported that 160,000 people had visited the Reading Room and that loan queues formed daily outside the library.

It didn't stay a lending library for long as the books weren't being brought back on time, so it's now a reference library but open to all (no membership required).

Lectures in the Great Hall were often quite unique, including titles such as 'Men I wish I'd

BISHOPSGATE
INSTITUTE

LETTS
DESK
DIARY
1952
WITH MONTHLY
ACCIDENT SECTION
Charles Letts & Co
COLLINS
ONE DAY
ROYAL
DIARY
1953
No. 53
Bower Ho...
COLLINS
ONE DAY
ROYAL
DIARY
1954
No. 53
COLLINS
LETTS
DESK
DIARY
1956
WITH MONTHLY CASH
ACCOUNT SECTION
No. - 21Z
Charles Letts & Co
DIARY HOUSE, LONDON, S.E.1

never met' and 'Misadventures of a Donkey.'
Sadly, no transcripts are available.

The educational classes were initially focused
on self-improvement subjects such as
bookkeeping and shorthand, whereas now,
it is much more aimed towards leisure and
enjoyment.

Stunning Building

When you first notice the building on
Bishopsgate, the foremost thought is often how
out of place the Grade II* listed structure now
looks with all the modern construction in the
City of London. But London is wonderful for
these juxtapositions, isn't it?

Charles Harrison Townsend (1851–1928) was
the architect, and he included elements of Arts
& Crafts and Art Nouveau styles, as well as
Romanesque and Byzantine influences too. The
green tiles on the corridor walls reminded me
of the Leslie Green tiles at tube stations such
as Regent's Park and Holloway Road. Townsend
went on to design two further major London
public buildings: the Whitechapel Art Gallery
(1901) and the Horniman Museum (1901).

The library still has the original wooden
shelving and original Librarian desk. There's also
an ornate stained-glass dome that was added in
the 1911 extension.

But while it might look somewhat intimidating,
this is not a stuffy place. You don't have to
whisper, although it is quiet so people can study
and read.

Charles Goss

The first librarian was Ronald Heaton, but
he didn't stay for long. His replacement was
Charles William Frederick Goss, who was Head

Librarian from 1897 to 1941. And he had a huge
impact here.

Goss was a fanatical book collector, buying
extensively at auction and from antiquarian
dealers. He had a keen interest in local
history, and he wasted no time in building up
a magnificent collection on the history and
topography of the inner London area. He read
them all so if you had a question about London,
he was the man to go to.

He was thorough as he acquired every
edition of John Stow's 'A Survey of London'
from the first published in 1598. (This is a
comprehensive topographical and historical
record of London's buildings, social conditions,
and customs at the time.) Plus a wonderful
collection of books written by overseas visitors
to London recounting their opinions on the
city. He was especially interested in London
directories, so ensured the library had a full
set of the Kelly's Directory from the 1700s
onwards. (It's a trade directory that listed all
businesses and tradespeople in a particular city
or town, as well as a general directory of postal
addresses of local gentry, landowners, charities,
and other facilities.)

Special Collections

The first special collection came to the Institute
in 1905 with the acquisition of the personal
library of George Howell, who had been MP
for Bethnal Green North-East in the 1880s.
Howell had been active in the early trade union
movement, and the collection includes the
Minute Book of the First International Working
Men's Association (1866–69) when Karl Marx
attended. This had to be locked away in a bank
vault for 25 years as there was fear it was some
sort of blueprint for communism and would
cause a revolution. But when it was released, at
the order of Prime Minister Winston Churchill,
it turned out just to have the sort of normal

meeting minutes of any association (attendees, who asked a question, etc.).

In 1906, the Institute acquired half of the personal library of George Jacob Holyoake, the pioneer of the Co-operative Movement, and this confirmed a need for extra space, so an extension was added to the library, opened in 1911.

Jack The Ripper & Crime

This area of London is synonymous with Jack the Ripper, so the library has about 250 books on the subject on the shelves. When I was surprised at the amount, we went into a back room where there were 1,000 more! These extras – along with board games, films, beer bottles, music, etc. with Jack the Ripper connections – were all left in a legacy from a chap who had often mentioned that he had more Ripper books than the library and felt Bishopsgate was the right place to hold his lifetime's collection. A true obsession if ever there was one.

There's also the family archive of Detective Inspector Frederick Wensley (1865–1949), who worked in Whitechapel and went on to be the Chief Constable of Scotland Yard Criminal Investigation Department. He worked on the Jack the Ripper murders, the Siege of Sidney Street, and the Houndsditch Murders.

Wensley liked to keep every press clipping about himself, lovingly pasted in scrapbooks with neat handwriting noting the date and publication. After he retired, he wrote his memoirs and enjoyed explaining how he solved the crimes in national newspaper exposés. As Stefan and I discussed, his life would make an excellent Sunday night TV crime drama series.

Someone who didn't get on well with "Weazel Wensley" was East End gangster Arthur Harding. Harding wrote his autobiography 'An Apprenticeship of Crime,' and his typed manuscript, with a wallpaper cover to protect it, is kept here. Historian Raphael Samuel interviewed Harding in the 1970s and later published 'East End Underworld: Chapters in the Life of Arthur Harding.' The recorded interviews are here in the archive too.

The Archives

Stefan opened plan chest drawers to show me marvelous maps of the area from the 1500s to today, and there's even every edition of the London A-Z – the street-finder book we all used before Google maps. The impressive London travel guide collection made me want to check for any missing against my many shelves of London books at home.

Filing cabinets are full of press cuttings as Goss kept anything that mentioned the City of London and surrounding areas. And there's an extensive pamphlet and leaflet collection too.

The collections are added to nearly every day as Stefan manages the largest collection of east London pizza delivery leaflets. It would be easy to dismiss these are 'straight to recycling' rubbish, but in years to come, these will show our time in history.

And that's what the Bishopsgate Institute special collections are about: the real social and cultural history of London, with particular reference to Bishopsgate and Spitalfields. Through these archives, we can discover all major aspects of the character of London and its social, economic, and architectural development.

Photography

There's a major collection of street

photography here with some of the most loved images by C. A. Mathew, a studio photographer from Essex who took some fascinating photos of the streets near the Bishopsgate Institute in 1912. The images have been scanned and restored so you can read the detail in shop windows and see the expressions on the faces of the children who came out to see this photographer at work. These really are wonderfully evocative images that make you feel like you're there. While we don't know why a studio photographer took these images, there are notes on the photos mentioning the road widths, so it may have been a commission for the local council or a developer.

And for proof that we are a nation of animal lovers, there's Libby Hall's collection of dog photography. This includes many lovely Victorian posed family photos with pet dogs included.

More Highlights

A more recent acquisition is the nearby Sandy Row Synagogue's archive. These record books had been stored in a damp basement so are not in the best condition, but they are an important archive and will be conserved soon.

The family archive of Bernie Grant, one of the first black British MPs, includes the robes he wore to the State Opening of Parliament, plus his Nokia mobile phone and his Sony Walkman.

Another wonderful collection held here is that of Agnes Dawson. She was a woman's suffrage campaigner and was instrumental in getting the law changed, so women teachers did not have to give up work when they got married. Her family donated her Women's Social and Political Union (WSPU) tea set and her 'Votes for Women' sashes. Yes, other London museums have these types of items, but this is the only place you can walk in and ask to see them without an appointment.

Bishopsgate Institute is building a 'Protest and Campaigning' special collection, so lots of placards taken on recent marches are leaning against the walls in one archive room. And there's also a 'Lesbian Gay Bisexual Transgender and Queer History' special collection too.

Great Diary Project

This is a national archive stored here with the diaries of 12,000 ordinary people from 1732 to today. If you want to know what a teenage boy was up to in east London in the 1950s, then you can now find out. They welcome diaries from any UK residents who want their ramblings to be kept forever. There's even a box of diaries labeled 'Confidential. Do not open until 2055'. Who knows the secrets that may hold.

I did ask if overseas visitors could get involved and, while you won't have diaries from living in the UK, your travel journal donations from trips to London would be welcome.

Why Are Special Collections Here?

You may well ask, why do people choose to give their family archives to the Bishopsgate Institute? The British Library or the Museum of London may also have been considered, but here the archives remain accessible. They are treasured and looked after. Everything is on-site and can be requested and brought to a desk for anyone to view. You don't need to be a library member to come here, and it's completely free to request to see items from the archives.

Seriously, what's not to love? I think I've found my new London happy place.

ALONG TH
Top 10 Things To See
By Joh

THE THAMES
ALONG THE THAMES PATH
RABON

Certainly one of the finest walking paths in the United Kingdom, the Thames Path stretches for 184 miles from the river's source in the Cotswolds to the Thames Flood Barrier in East London. No matter how long you travel on it, it's a beautiful path through one of England's most beautiful places to the very heart of Britain's capital. Of course, you don't need to walk the full length of the Thames Path to enjoy it. If you find yourself in London, you can follow it from the moment it enters the city until its end. We have identified ten different things you can see along the Thames Path in London.

Hampton Court Palace

Right along the Thames, one of the first places you'll want to see is Hampton Court Palace. It was originally built around 1515 for Cardinal Thomas Wolseley, but after he fell out of favor, King Henry VIII took it for himself as recompense for Wolseley's disgrace. It ended up being his favorite royal residence, and while still the property of the Crown, it also operates as a museum. It has wonderful decorative chimneys, a Tudor-style roasting hearth in the kitchens, a timber-beamed great hall, and more. A 17th Century aborted renovation left it with some Baroque features as well, making for an interesting hodge-podge of styles.

Kew Gardens

Kew Gardens is one of the largest and most diverse botanical gardens in the world, with over 30,000 different species of plant spread out over 300 acres. In the middle of all this is Kew Palace, a royal palace that has been home to Robert Dudley, Queen Charlotte, and the children of King George II. The Dutch House is all that remains of the original palace, but it is still worth seeing for its historical value, and paired with the Royal Botanic Gardens, you could spend an entire day here.

Battersea Park

One of the largest green spaces along the River Thames at 200 acres, Battersea Park, is a top destination for those looking for some gorgeous nature. There's so much to do in the park that it could almost make for its own top ten articles. Whether you're going for the greenery, the Children's Zoo, the Peace Pagoda, the bandstand, the Pump House Gallery, or more, you'll find this is a great place to spend the day.

Houses of Parliament and Big Ben

Located right next to the river, the Palace of Westminster has been home to the government since it was the palace of Canute the Great. The first Parliament (or "Model Parliament") met here in 1295, and it became their home after King Henry VIII vacated it for the Palace of Whitehall. The current building dates from the 19th Century after a fire destroyed the original Houses of Parliament. While most people refer to the tower as Big Ben, the name actually refers to the bell inside, and the tower itself is named Elizabeth Tower for Queen Elizabeth II.

London Eye

One of the best ways to see the Thames and the city is high atop a flight on the London Eye. A thirty-minute ride on this cantilevered Ferris wheel is a thrilling experience and one of the highest views of London you're going to get. The London Eye also offers special flights for a little extra and be sure to buy your tickets in advance as it is a very popular attraction.

Shakespeare's Globe

Right alongside the river in Southbank, Shakespeare's Globe was the dream of Sam Wanamaker, who sought to build a faithful recreation of the Elizabethan venue in Southbank. This end result is so faithful that it also doubles as a museum where visitors can take tours to learn more about the Bard and theatre performances of his era. In addition to the regular series of Shakespearean plays featured in the Globe's schedule, the venue also sees other surviving plays from the era and newer historical dramas.

Tower Bridge

One of the most famous bridges connecting the banks of the River Thames, Tower Bridge is an excellent example of Gothic Revival architecture in the city. It is also one of the most famous examples of a bascule bridge, built to cater to the increasing traffic along the river. If you ever visit, be sure to go up to the pedestrian foot tunnel for one of the best views of the Thames you'll get.

Cutty Sark

While many ships are docked along the Thames, none are so grand as the Cutty Sark. It's one of the last tall ships left intact in the United Kingdom, and during its lifetime, the ship was a fast clipper that brought tea from China back to Britain. Now it exists as a museum that lets people see what it was really like to sail on a 19th Century vessel. You can even go under the ship to view its magnificent hull for yourself.

The O2 Arena

Opened originally as an exhibition center, it proved to be a financial flop until it was revitalized into a sporting and concert venue. The brave can venture to the top for one of the best views of the city through Up at O2. There's also a bowling alley, movie theater, and even an exhibition center.

Thames Barrier

The Thames Barrier serves an important purpose for the city in helping to prevent flooding from the River Thames. Of course, the artful design of the flood control measures makes them a tourist destination themselves. They also mark the end of the Thames Path, and you can either choose to begin your wandering here or end your walk.

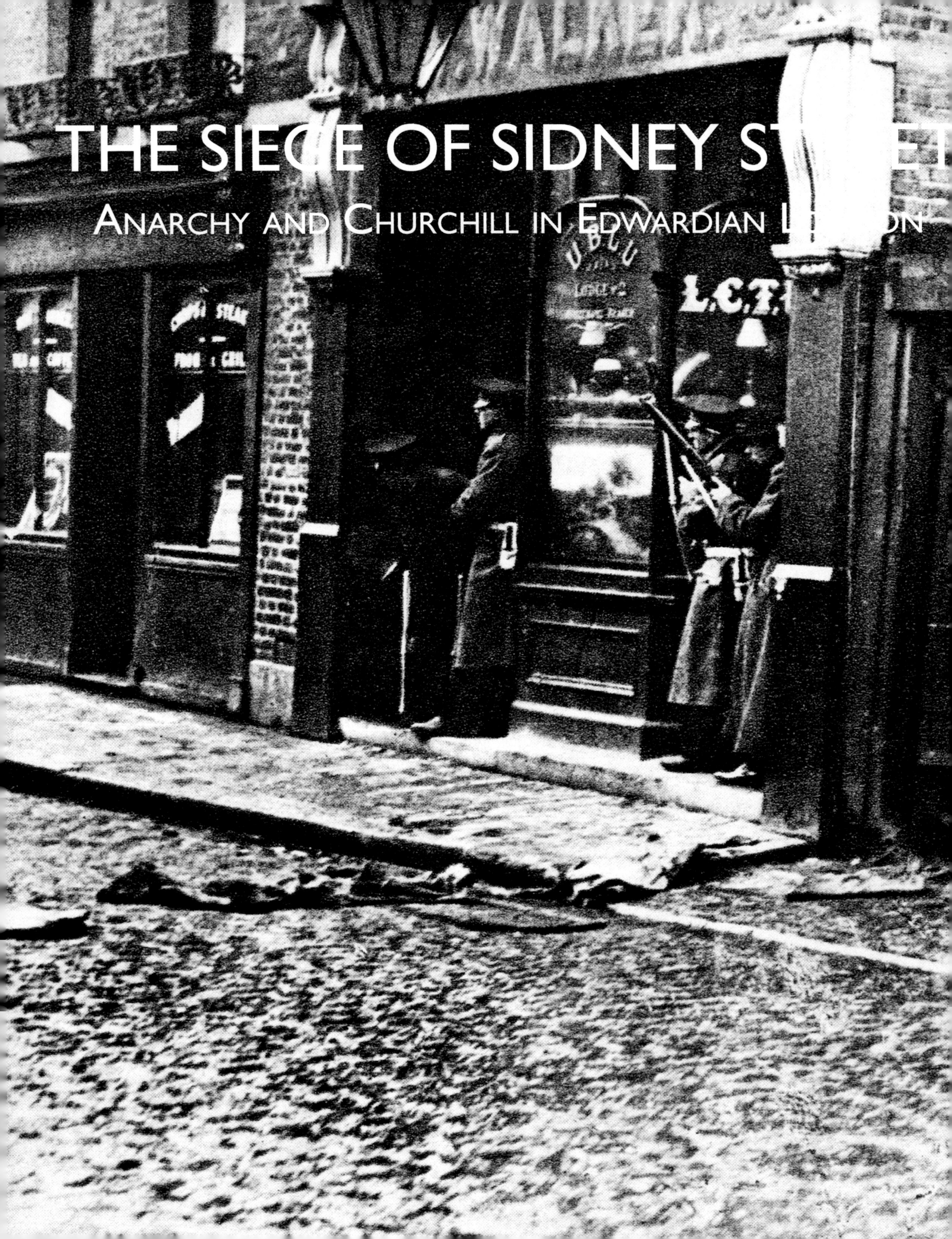
THE SIEGE OF SIDNEY STREET
ANARCHY AND CHURCHILL IN EDWARDIAN LONDON

Chronicle
BEST FOR
NEWS
RS.
RS.
RS.
T FOR
WS.
FOR
TS.

When you think of London, it is unlikely you will picture dramatic gunfights in the streets or an armed gang of Latvian revolutionaries being hunted by the police, but that's the reality of events during the Siege of Sidney Street in the winter of 1911.

See, over the years, the East End of London has grown notorious for its criminal activity. Starting in the Victorian era, the Ratcliff Highway murders of 1811 led to seven fatalities, and later that century, Jack the Ripper, a serial killer, took the lives of five women in the same area. Crime continued well into the next decade, and in the 1950s and 60s, the Kray Twins terrorized the area with the criminal empire they established. Today, though some parts of the East End are rapidly changing, unfortunately, it still contains some of the worst poverty in the country, and this is linked to high levels of crime in the area too.

The Siege of Sidney Street all started when Latvian revolutionaries murdered three policemen during a jewelry shop robbery gone wrong, known today as the Houndsditch murders. After finding two of the gang members hiding away in a building on Sidney Street a month later, a gunfight broke out in the streets among the police and gang members. Eventually, the building caught on fire, and the two gang members inside died. It provoked a national debate about whether the police in London ought to be armed, how many immigrants/ refugees should be allowed into the country, and the perils of socialism and anarchism.

Background

Between 1875 and 1914, faced with religious persecution and pogroms, approximately 120,000 Jews emigrated from the Russian Empire to the UK. Large numbers of these settled in London's East End, including Houndsditch and Whitechapel. By 1910, many

of these individuals gathered at the Anarchist Club in Jubilee Street – though you did not have to be an anarchist to attend.

The small group who became involved in the events at both Houndsditch and Sidney Street were Latvians, and not all anarchists even though such literature was distributed among them. Historian Bernard Porter speculates that those in the group were all likely revolutionaries, though radicalized by their experiences in Russia and of the belief one was valid in expropriating private property for the greater good. It should be noted too that none of those associated with the 'gang' involved were Jewish, yet their links to the large numbers of recently immigrated Jewish people unfairly increased tension and suspicion of Jewish people in the area.

Houndsditch Murders

In December 1910, Henry Samuel Harris owned 119 Houndsditch, a jeweler's shop, which backed onto a small cul-de-sac with accommodation for rent called the Exchange Buildings. The Latvian gang, who estimated a safe inside contained between £20,000 and £30,000 worth of jewelry, started to rent property in the Exchange Buildings, including number 9 and 11. Unfortunately for the criminals, they were unable to rent number 10, directly behind their target. However, over the period of two weeks, they brought various tools and equipment to help carry out

a heist at the jewelry shop, and number 10 lay unoccupied from the 12 December.
On 16 December, around 10 pm that evening, Max Weil heard loud noises from his neighbor's property. As it happens, he found Police Constable Piper on his beat outside his house and told him about the strange noises. Upon further investigation, PC Piper knocked on 11 Exchange Buildings and grew increasingly suspicious, venturing to nearby Bishopsgate Police Station to report the situation. By 11:30 pm, nine policemen gathered in the area, armed with wood truncheons.

Sergeant Robert Bentley knocked on the door of number 11, and after a little commotion, the back door opened, and a few members of the gang began firing pistols. One gang member shot Bentley in the shoulder and neck and severed his spine. Another member shot fellow police officer Bryant in the arm and chest and shot Woodhams in the leg.

As the gang escaped the building and made for the end of the road, other police officers present attempted to intervene. This led

Sergeant Charles Tucker to be hit twice; he died instantly. Sergeant Choate attempted to grab one of the gang members, wrestling over the gun, but ended up being shot in the leg then swiftly shot another twelve times by gang members who sought to save their fellow member from the police.

In the end, Tucker, Choate, and Bentley all died, the largest multiple murder of police officers carried out in Britain during peacetime. While the other officers survived, neither Bryant nor Woodhams recovered fully from their injuries. Naturally, this horrific crime led to a widespread manhunt for the individuals responsible who had gone on the run after fleeing the scene.

Siege of Sidney Street

After receiving reliable information about the whereabouts of two men involved in the Houndsditch murders, Svaars and Sokoloff, just after midnight on 3 January 1911, two hundred police officers cordoned off the area around 100 Sidney Street. Other residents on the street were awoken and evacuated as the police suspected there was a high chance of a gang-related shootout.

Just after 7:30 am, police managed to wake the two gang members, and upon appearing at the window, they seized the opportunity to open fire at police. Their shots wounded a police sergeant, and while some returned fire, their guns proved ineffective over such a great range. Knowing the two gunmen possessed superior weapons, the officers obtained permission from Winston Churchill, Home Secretary, to bring in a military detachment of the Scots Guards.

For some reason, in a matter that still puzzles historians, Winston Churchill appeared at the Siege too. Although he states he did not make any police decisions, when shooting between

SDITCH
EXCHANGE BUILDINGS
No 9. USED BY BURGLARS.
No 10. EMPTY.
No 11. WHERE BURGLARS LIVED — SCENE OF SHOOTING
BACK OF Mr HARRIS'S SHOP
YARD

the two sides stopped and smoke was seen coming from the second-floor window around 12:50, Churchill supported the police decision to refuse access by the London Fire Brigade present at the scene.

By 2:30 pm, the shooting stopped, and it became clear the men inside were dead. At this point, Churchill allowed the fire brigade to start extinguishing the flames to prevent it from spreading to further buildings. Sadly, when the firemen entered the building and extracted the bodies, a wall collapsed on five of them, one of whom died six months after the Siege from his injuries.

Aftermath

Winston Churchill's presence at the scene was questioned by many, and it was felt he was putting lives in unnecessary danger by being present at the scene. Today, many think the reasoning for his being there is simply because he was intrigued by what was going on and wanted to witness the action, regardless of the consequences it may have had.

Once located, police arrested the rest of the gang, some of whom were discharged on the basis of insufficient evidence while others, who took part in trials, ended in acquittal. The only person found guilty was Nina Vassilleva. However, the court overturned her conviction on appeal anyway.

Legacy

The use of guns in the Houndsditch murders made the case particularly notorious, given the usual lack of guns in British robberies. It provoked a national debate about whether the police in London ought to be armed. Further, the Liberal government revisited immigration law in the wake of the events as it was at a time when several 'immigrants,' now known as refugees, poured into Britain, and the status of those in the gang led to a nativist backlash, as well as uneasiness about foreign anarchism and socialism generally.

Sites to Visit

Note, while the original buildings involved were destroyed during World War Two, the street layout remains unaltered so you can follow in the footsteps of the officers' lives.

You can also find a memorial plaque for the three murdered policemen in Houndsditch, and one in honor of the fireman who died during the Sidney Siege.

Film & TV

- The Man Who Knew Too Much (1934, Hitchcock) – Ending inspired by the Siege.
- The Siege of Sidney Street (1960)

Further Research

- Book – The Siege of Sidney Street by F Oughton (1960)
- Book – A Death Out of Season by Emanuel Litvinoff (1973)

BEHIND THE SCENES AT 55 BROADWAY
London's First Skyscraper and London Underground's Headquarters
By Laura Porter

We've explored the Hidden London Tours operated by the London Transport Museum in the past on Anglotopia and Londontopia, this time we wanted to try something quite different, so instead of going underground, we joined a tour of London's first skyscraper, 55 Broadway, the former headquarters of Transport for London. TFL has since moved the building is now being turned into a hotel, so these final tours back in 2019 were a rare chance to see the building before it was renovated.

NEW HEADQUARTERS NEEDED

The Underground Group, also known as the Underground Electric Railways of London, had enlarged their offices a few times, including extending over the railway tracks of St James's Park station in 1922. More space was still needed, so Frank Pick (1878–1941), Managing Director of the UERL commissioned the architect Charles Holden (1875–1960) of the firm Adams Holden and Pearson to design the building.

The headquarters was to symbolize the company's vision of public transport being at the heart of London's social and commercial life. At the time, this was a profit-driven, private company and not a government body.

CHARLES HOLDEN

In 1923, Pick commissioned Holden to design a façade for a side entrance at Westminster Underground station. This was followed in 1924 with designs for seven new stations in south London for the extension of the City and South London Railway (now part of the Northern line). The designs reflected the simple modernist style Holden was using in France for war cemeteries, and each was well-adapted to suit the street corner sites of most of the

stations.

In 1926, Holden began the design of a new headquarters for the UERL at 55 Broadway above St. James's Park station.

ST JAMES'S PARK STATION

St James's Park station has been here since 1868 as a station on the Metropolitan District Railway (known simply as the District Railway, the precursor to the District Line). The railway line runs diagonally underneath 55 Broadway, and the whole building straddles the station, the east and west wings being immediately above the railway tunnel.

CRUCIFORM SHAPE

The irregular 'kite-shaped' footprint brought its own challenges. Holden used the full space for the first two levels and then designed a cruciform plan above. Pick was adamant that the building design should be led by its use and be 'fit for purpose,' which is what led to the great need for natural light in the offices.

Open-plan offices radiate in four wings from a central tower, and there are no internal light wells. This plan followed contemporary American office design but was considered an innovation in London in the 1920s.

STEEL FRAME

55 Broadway was never the tallest building in London, even when it was first built. (For example, nearby 'Big Ben' is 315 feet/96 m high whereas 55 Broadway is 175 feet/53 m.) But it was London's first skyscraper as it used an encased steel frame technique that was pioneered by American skyscrapers, which encouraged growth upwards rather than outward. This might explain why some say the

55 Broadway
St. James's Park
London Underground
Limited
Head Office
Reception

TRAIN INTERVALS
DISTRICT
METROPOLITAN
NORTHERN LINE

building has a hint of the 'Gotham City' about it.

Each wing rises to 80 feet (the limit imposed by the 1894 Building Act) with the pitch of its set-back attic stories at the maximum permitted. The central clock tower goes much higher, but as it neither reduced the daylight of neighboring buildings nor disrupted the streetscape, the restrictions were waved. In the center, under the tower, is the vertical circulation of lifts and the main staircase.

By choosing a tapered silhouette – the 7th, 9th, and the 10th stories are stepped back – Holden could have more height reaching to 14 stories (the top 4 stories are in the tower) as there were fewer people at higher levels, which were the emergency evacuation concerns. (Restrictions prevented the floors above the 7th from being used as offices.) This was made possible as the external walls are not load-bearing as the building uses a structural steel frame for support.

The planning owes much to Holden's earlier work on hospital buildings, where issues of cross-ventilation were paramount and courtyard plans discouraged. The General Motors Building in Detroit, which Holden's partner Pearson photographed on a trip to America, also influenced the design.

Several hundred reinforced-concrete piles underpin the building with 19 load-bearing steel girders providing support across the railway tracks and platforms of St James's Station below.

The exterior is clad in 2200 m2 of unpolished Portland stone. This gives 55 Broadway a grand, yet slightly rugged appearance compared to other notable structures such as Buckingham Palace or the National Gallery in Trafalgar Square, which are finished in the same material.

Upon completion, this was the tallest steel-framed office building in London until construction of another Holden building, the University of London's Senate House (based on similar designs and materials).

AWARD-WINNING

The Underground Group headquarters at 55 Broadway opened on 1 December 1929 and was clearly a sleek, modern and efficient building. The desire to make a bold architectural statement in keeping with the ideals of the company had been realized.

In its opening year, this statement building was awarded the Royal Institute of British Architects London Architecture Medal. (You can see the medal above the entrance facing Tothill Street.)

SCANDALOUS SCULPTURES

While the building's modern design avoided over-adornment, Holden did commission seven of Britain's leading avant-garde artists to create ten larger-than-life sculptures across the building's exterior.

Having admired Jacob Epstein's highly-controversial sculpture on Percy Adams' British Medical Association building, Holden commissioned Epstein to produce two figurative sculptures for the lower levels. He also commissioned six other prominent sculptors: Eric Gill, Allan Wyon, Henry Moore, Samuel Rabinovitch, Eric Aumonier, and Alfred Gerrard to work on higher-level sculptures. Holden's brief required the figures to be 'carved direct in the stone without the mechanical means of reproduction,' so scaffolding went up for the artists to work in situ.

Jacob Epstein's 'Night' and 'Day' sculptural reliefs caused the most controversy. 'Night' is a

METROPOLITAN DISTRICT RAILWAY COMPANY
CONDITIONS AS TO
THE ISSUE OF TICKETS.

shrouded woman cradling a frail looking child. 'Day' is a seated adult male with a young boy whose penis becomes a central focal point of the work. Their primitive style and the figures' naked modernist glory created a furor. Calls to remove the sculptures were resisted by both Holden and Pick, who even offered to resign over this issue. A compromise was reached, and a 1.5-inch section of penis was chiseled off.

The other sculptors, led by Eric Gill, created eight bas-reliefs representing the four Winds (two for each of the cardinal directions, on each side of the projecting wings). These are on pediments above the sixth floor on each of the eight principal faces of the cruciform building. All eight are nude figures, positioned horizontally and facing the direction of the wind that they represent. Of particular note is Henry Moore's female relief representing the West Wind on the north side of the east wing as this was his first public commission.

GRADE I LISTED

The building was first listed as Grade II in 1970. In the 1980s, the ground floor offices were redesigned to create a new reception area and a shopping mall. It was upgraded to Grade I in 2011.

It has been listed for being a milestone in twentieth-century design, signaling the influence of America on British architecture. It was chosen as Holden's best building and for being a fine showcase of pre-Second World War British sculpture with the foremost artists of the period represented, including Jacob Epstein, Eric Gill, and Henry Moore.

THE TOUR

This Hidden London tour offers exclusive access to London Underground's iconic former headquarters. Numbers are limited, and you get to examine the Lobby, areas of the 2nd and 7th floors, and then journey up to the 10th and 14th floors for the outdoor areas. You'll also see a beautiful stairwell and hear from two expert Guides.

The 90-minute tour uses the lifts/elevators up to the 10th floor, and then there are stairs to get to the highest level.

Art Deco

The building has many Art Deco features, from the unpolished Italian Travertine marble walls and flooring to the bronze doors, ventilation grilles, and bronze window frames on the ground floor. There's even a bronze architrave around the lifts. There's a starburst motif over the entrance doors and original lighting in the Lobby ceiling.

Holden's attention to detail was incredible as he also designed the most elegant bronze door plates and even the door handles for the Chairman's Office on the 7th floor.

The Underground Company, along with many other large companies of the time, was very hierarchical. We compared the higher ceiling height between the 2nd and 7th floor to see that the Senior Directors were treated differently. The "corridor of power" towards the Chairman's Office has wood paneling with walnut doors leading to offices with Belgium black marble fireplaces. The Senior Executive offices each had a private bathroom with not just a toilet but a bath too. The Chairman's Office was used by Lord Ashfield as Chairman of London Transport and his successors until about 2006.

Clocks

Timekeeping is important to a transport company, so the electric clocks in the Lobby, and others on each floor of the building, were operated by a clock in the basement. As the tour takes you to the Clock Winding Room in the tower, you can see the building's tower clock is now digitally operated.

Train Indicator

On entering the ground floor reception of the building, there is an original Train Interval indicator. Each paper disc represents a tube line, and they were marked with an ink dot around the edges to show when a train passed through a designated point, showcasing the reliable service.

Drinking Fountains

Near the lifts on each floor, there is a drinking fountain that was fed by an artesian well under the building. Unfortunately, it was discovered in the 1970s that the water was not safe to drink even though the fountains had been in use for decades!

Tenth Floor

This was the Board members and Directors Dining Suite but is now a function suite. At this level, there are four roof terraces, and we went out onto Meadow Terrace to get a closer look at the tower clock and for those amazing views over London. This terrace has a wildflower meadow and solar panels too.

The Top

The lift only reaches the 10th floor, so from here, we climbed the stairs up to the Clock Winding Room that is on the 12th and 13th floors. (No floor was designated as the 13th floor.) The final ascent to the 14th-floor rooftop viewing area above the clock is via a narrow metal staircase but safe and totally worth the climb as you reach the very top of the building! There is a huge wow factor looking out over Westminster with the Shard in the background and the London Eye clear to see. The green expanse of St. James's Park provides a contrast with the built city, and you can even see Crystal Palace in south London in the distance.

Stairwell

The journey back to ground level is all via stairs. We had the option to get the lift from the 10th floor, but everyone chose to take the stairs as they are definitely worth seeing.

The attention to detail includes fluted-design balustrades (steel, not bronze this time) and green chevron tiles pointing the way down. A lot of consideration was used for what is essentially a fire escape.

The area has plenty of natural light, and the walk down is broken up, admiring old transport signs that have been added. There's an Underground map that looks like a real tangle as it's geographical and not the simplified Harry Beck diagram that came a year later in 1931. You can see a map just like this on display at Temple tube station.

THE BUILDING'S FUTURE

In early 2017, Transport for London dropped plans to sell 55 Broadway for luxury residential redevelopment. Instead, TfL continued using the offices and then sold a long-term lease for commercial development. TfL admitted 55 Broadway was no longer 'fit for purpose.' They will not become luxury apartments; however, in 2020, it was announced that it would become a hotel, so anyone who stays there will get to experience the majesty of this building.

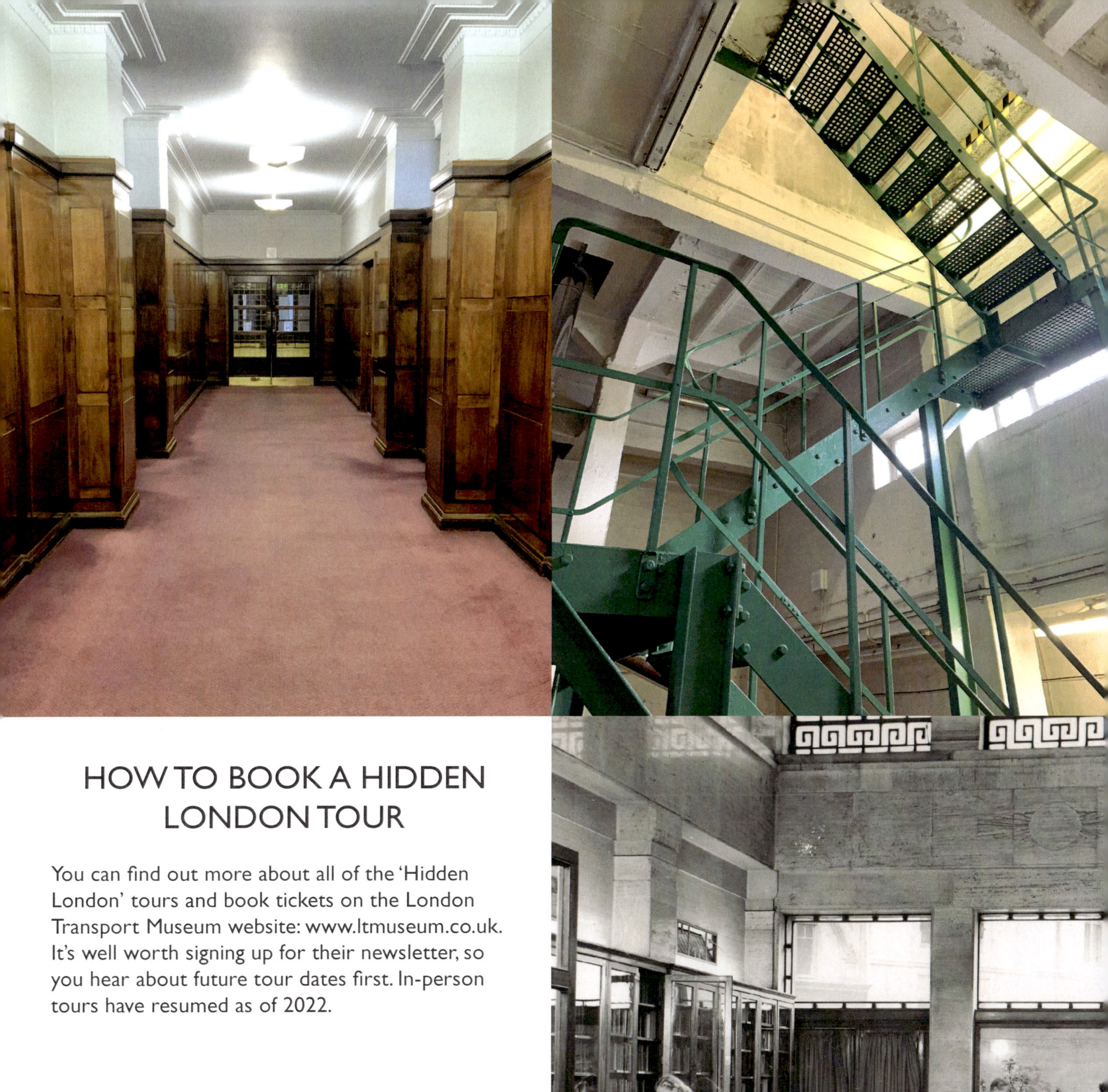

HOW TO BOOK A HIDDEN LONDON TOUR

You can find out more about all of the 'Hidden London' tours and book tickets on the London Transport Museum website: www.ltmuseum.co.uk. It's well worth signing up for their newsletter, so you hear about future tour dates first. In-person tours have resumed as of 2022.

HOW COVID HAS CHANGED LONDON
By Laura Porter

There must be nowhere on earth unaffected by the pandemic, but what changes has it meant for London? During the lockdowns, we had a variety of government dictates with catchy slogans. 'Stay local' has had a long-lasting effect as central London does not yet have the same atmosphere we enjoyed in pre-Covid days.

I remember in February 2020 still going to two or three museums a week and catching up with friends and family at the weekend. I didn't question getting on public transport and didn't own a car as it wasn't necessary. I would hug my friends and shake hands with business contacts. But we soon all became trained to keep our distance at all times.

The enforced rules did change our habits and has left us with a level of anxiety and underlying intolerance. Whether to wear face masks or not has divided Londoners, as it has for people across the globe. We are a nation of rebels, so there was always going to be a time when it would be harder to ensure all complied.

STAY LOCAL

After 'Stay home,' the rule was 'Stay local' so Londoners got to know their neighborhoods better. Those who previously commuted to work every day and never saw their local shops got to see which businesses survived on their local High Street. Sadly, with the risk of shortages and the need for social distancing, food shopping that once could have meant friendly conversations with local shopkeepers soon became something to endure.

For many, the area close to their home has become the size of their world. We didn't all jump to get back to central London once allowed, and there has been ongoing

trepidation. For those of us that love London, it has been hard to hear about the number of closures and to adapt to the new norm. The capital has become a city that requires more planning and less spontaneity.

I have a well-trained lack of FOMO (Fear Of Missing Out) as there has always been so much choice in London that you have to start to slow down eventually. But I have been much more reluctant to travel into central London (I live in zone 3) even with the draw of blockbuster exhibitions at the major museums.

WORKING FROM HOME

It's going to be hard to persuade office workers to return to commuting to central London five days a week when it's now been proven that staff at home can be relied upon to get the job done. Some businesses are encouraging a mix of home and office workdays as not everyone has a suitable working environment at home, and many have missed their colleagues. But the futility and cost of commuting have not been missed.

Long term, businesses will continue to not renew leases on office space, and large work-space tower blocks will need repurposing soon, adding to the empty building issues.

Fewer workers in town mean London is generally quieter. And the lack of international tourism has clearly had an impact too. But it definitely felt busier in central London during summer 2021 compared to summer 2020. There was some of the buzz and atmosphere back.

How things will change in 2022 once we enter a new phase of the pandemic, remains to be seen. A large number of people will probably remain working from home or adapt to 'hybrid' working arrangements where they go into the office a couple days of the week.

PUBLIC TRANSPORT

Central London is not somewhere you drive to with the Congestion Charge and lack of parking. We have a considerable network of public transport, and that's how 99% of Londoners get into town. But many of us are still thinking twice before hopping on any form of public transport and have a healthy aversion to unnecessary travel. Some confided to feeling 'a bit freaked out' on a hot and crowded tube after so long, maintaining social distancing, which is a very relatable experience.

I've noticed on the tube, people prefer not to touch the hold bars. And personal space is even more important as no one wants to sit next to a stranger. But it's getting busier, so there are times when every seat is taken, and all standing areas are full too. And that's not just during the rush hours. The visual assault of signs and notices on the tube now include "Please keep your distance" and other social distancing reminders that are near impossible to adhere to in a busy carriage.

Those wearing masks give 'looks' to those who don't. There is a 'Condition of Carriage' to wear a face mask unless exempt, but no one is stopped as they enter, so maskless travel is not confronted. It sometimes feels as if the looks of frustration, anger, and defiance are now standard, and people seem less tolerant.

CULTURAL SPONTANEITY

The simple pleasure of walking into any public arts institution without the faff of booking a ticket has long gone. Now, even for free museums, you generally need to pre-book a ticket online for a timed entry. The reason is for 'capacity management' but there is a cautious concern these days that some museums may be using it as an excuse for collecting our data during the online registration.

TRACK AND TRACE

The desire to leave "Track and Trace" contact details has reduced after the news was full of early summer "pingdemic" stories. While the media led with the story that too many "healthy" people were being made to isolate after close contact, it changed the nation's attitude to wanting to be wrongly pinged (alerted by the NHS Covid app and forced to stay home for up to 10 days). The rules changed (again) to state that you only have to isolate after close contact if you have symptoms. That rather ruined the app's intention, which was to stop the virus from being spread by those who had it but did not yet have symptoms. Anyway, it'll likely all have changed again when we reach our publication date, but I doubt most people will be convinced to check in and give contact details when going for a pint, for dinner, or to see an exhibition. I'm certainly less willing to check in on the app these days in case I'm wrongly sent an alert.

RESTAURANT BOOKING

Booking ahead for restaurants has never been more important. Lost is the excitement of finding a new place to eat when you can't just walk in and need to book for another day. Even if you look in the window and there is space, you are likely to be asked to get out your phone and book a table online to be allowed to enter (remember that joy of data capture again). It does take away a lot of the delight of discovering somewhere new for dinner.

And don't forget to cancel your booking in good time if you can't make it as some restaurants are receiving full house bookings only for the no-shows leaving them with many empty tables.

You can still have a spontaneous trip to the pub or a cafe, and you are encouraged to check-in or leave your contact details when you enter.

PEDESTRIAN-FRIENDLY

As 'daily exercise' became a thing, more cycle lanes were added to roads to encourage more to go for a bike ride. Some roads have been closed off to traffic to create pedestrian-only zones making it much nicer as a pedestrian these days.

Going for a walk is a much more popular pastime than before, but whereas I may have previously chosen to walk the streets of central London, I now choose quieter areas nearer to home.

The traffic-free zones have allowed much more outdoor dining. Areas such as Old Compton Street in Soho have a new lease of life with tables for drinking and dining outside all day and all evening.

CONCLUSION

I think my appraisal could sound mostly doom and gloom, but there has been resilience to not taking life for granted and for making the best of a situation. There have been adjustments, and London is still here. We may just need to adapt to the new London of today.

This was written in September 2021, so things may have changed again by publication and again by the time you read.

TELEPHONE
TELEPHONE
TELEPHONE
TELEPHONE
TELEPHONE